HEALTHY Air Fryer COOKBOOK

ALPHA

HEALTHY
Air Fryer
COOKBOOK

100 great recipes with fewer calories and less fat!

Dana Angelo White, MS, RD, ATC

Contents

Wholesome Snacks 107

(Less) Sinful Desserts 135

Introduction

I'm a registered dietitian and a die-hard foodie, but I wouldn't blame you for thinking these two disciplines don't have much in common.

Long before I got into nutrition, I was raised to appreciate the power of home cooking: that preparing a meal is love, is family, is joy. Later in life, I was lucky enough to pursue an education in nutrition—a journey that taught me that healthy food is *real* food. I learned that it takes little more than fresh ingredients and simple steps to make a tasty meal. But as a mom of three, my definition of healthy also needs to include being fast!

A stigma exists in my personal and professional worlds: People suspect I don't eat pizza or burgers or sugar. The truth is, I do … but in small amounts, and if I can use what I've learned to make certain foods delicious and better for me, then I'm all for it.

Creating this book was a culinary boot camp of sorts, particularly getting to know the ins and outs of the air fryer and discovering new ways I could use it. I admit, I was skeptical at first and questioned whether this machine has a real purpose beyond low-fat French fries. I'm very selective with my kitchen gadgets and wasn't sure it was worth the countertop real estate—until I started to use it.

But more than 100 recipes later, this powerful appliance continues to impress me, and I'm proud to share the final results with you. I want everyone who reads and tries these recipes to explore what the air fryer can do and where it can do it: anywhere with an electrical outlet. Cooking on family camping trips and in studio apartments and college dorm rooms just got a lot more interesting.

> **… if I can use what I've learned to make certain foods delicious and better for me, then I'm all for it.**

What makes the recipes in this book truly healthy is portion control. You can still enjoy donuts, pizza, and French fries, but those *real* ingredients in moderation and in smaller portions will benefit you and your health. This also means less fat, less sodium, and, yes, fewer calories.

Use the air fryer to create easy weekday meals for the family or fun finger food for company. You'll find ideas for every occasion—from play dates to game day. A healthy day in the life of the air fryer kitchen might start with huevos rancheros for breakfast and lead to a Caesar salad with kale and homemade croutons for lunch. Whatever you decide to make, please don't forget the occasional sweet treat. Make summertime strawberry shortcake at the peak of berry season or some zeppole with cannoli dip—the surprise favorite of my three daughters!

Whatever you create in the air fryer, make it fun, make it fast—and make it delicious!

Dana White

— *Dana Angelo White*

Acknowledgments

Creating this book has been nothing short of a culinary adventure. Every day, I set off to explore new territory, dreaming up how to use an air fryer in ways I never thought possible.

This process was a joyride in large part to the help, guidance, and organizational skills of Christopher Stolle, Brook Farling, and the entire team at Alpha and DK. Many thanks to Carolyn Doyle for getting her hands dirty testing recipes and providing invaluable feedback to make the final product something I'm truly proud of.

My recipes would never be complete without my four experienced and adorable recipe testers: Zack, Madeline, Charlotte, and Isla. Thank you for tasting my creations and always being cheerfully (and sometimes brutally) honest. You're my heart and soul and make me a better chef every day.

Publisher's Acknowledgments

The publisher would like to thank JD Schuyler for his lighting work and Rana Salame Striedinger for her help with food styling.

About the Author

Dana Angelo White, MS, RD, ATC, is a registered dietitian and nutrition consultant. Dana is the founder and president of Dana White Nutrition, specializing in media nutrition and recipe development. She's also the nutrition expert for FoodNetwork.com, the founding contributor for the website's Healthy Eats blog, and the author of *First Bites: Superfoods for Babies and Toddlers* (Perigee, 2015).

AIR FRYER BASICS

This chapter details how the air fryer works,
why air frying is better than deep frying, and how
to get the most out of this incredibly versatile appliance.

What Is Air Frying?

Air frying is a new way to cook healthier and faster. It cooks foods that might normally be deep fried, roasted, grilled, or baked by using convection heat to cook with less fat. The result is delicious food that's healthier because it contains less oil and fewer calories.

How It Works

Air frying takes conventional convection cooking to the next level. Air-fried food is cooked by circulating superheated air around the cooking chamber via a convection fan. The result is food that's delicious, crispy, and golden brown crust—and just as tasty as deep-fried food. Flavor is locked in, but because food cooks with little oil, the air fryer can make healthier versions of many of your fried favorites—and with fewer calories.

Although air frying food means somewhat longer cook times than deep-frying food, you'll feel better about the foods you eat when you realize you're consuming less fat, fewer calories, and more healthy ingredients. In fact, air frying often enables you to use many ingredients that are fresher and otherwise would not hold up under a deep fryer's high temperatures.

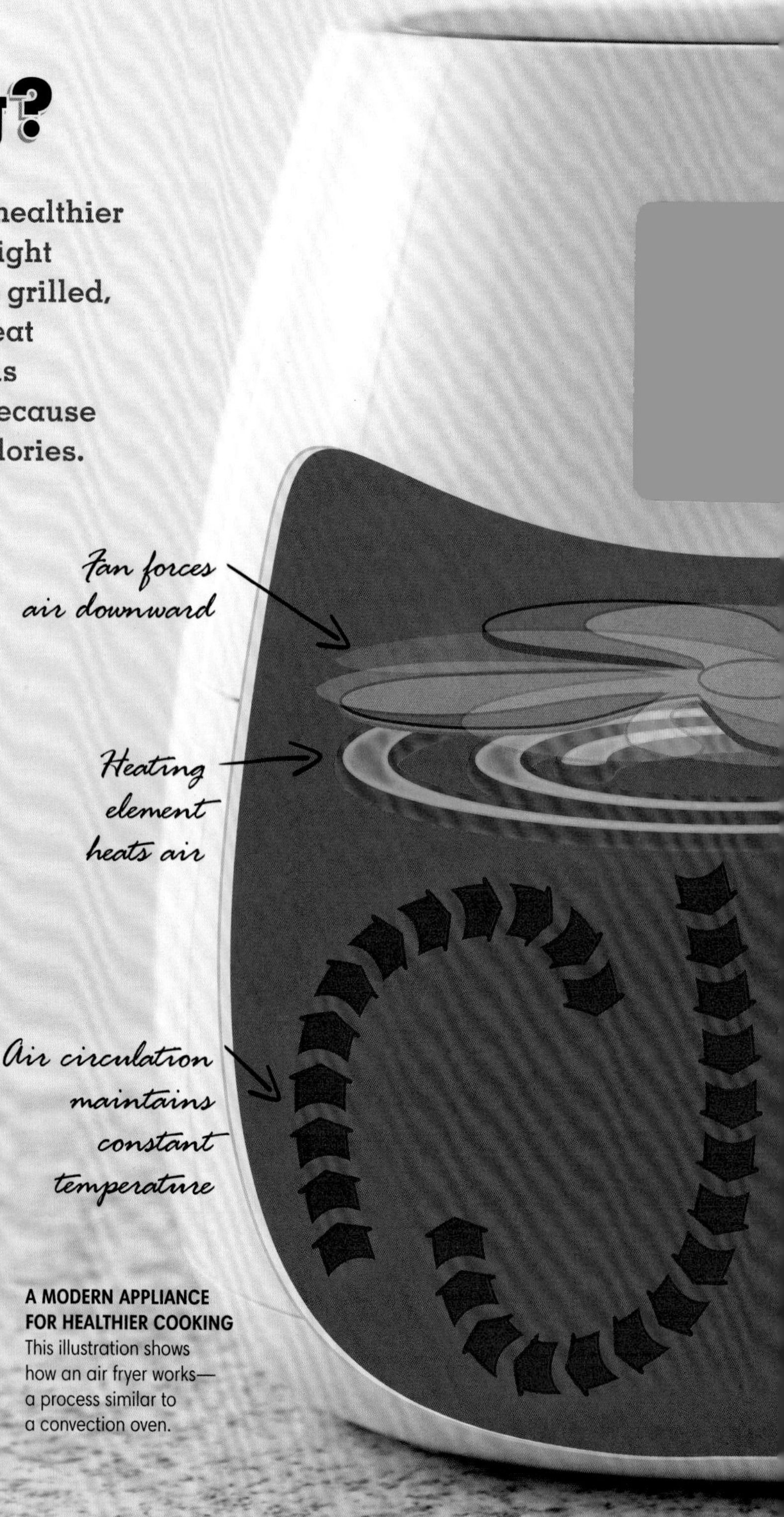

Fan forces air downward

Heating element heats air

Air circulation maintains constant temperature

A MODERN APPLIANCE FOR HEALTHIER COOKING
This illustration shows how an air fryer works— a process similar to a convection oven.

Why It's Better

Your air fryer does a lot more than just fry. It's an appliance you can use every day for all types of foods, and it can replace virtually any cooking appliance in your kitchen.

It's incredibly versatile

Not only can you air fry, but you can also bake, roast, and even grill in the air fryer. Most air fryer manufacturers offer a number of optional accessories—including nonstick baking and grill pans—that expand the versatility of your air fryer and enable you to make almost anything you might otherwise make with other appliances.

It's healthier

Air frying uses the convection process to cook foods. Convection circulates superheated air through the cooking chamber, resulting in food that not only includes less oil and fewer calories but also still seals in flavor and produces the crisp, crunchy texture that fried-food lovers crave.

Cleanup is a snap

Cleaning the air fryer is as simple as giving the interior a quick wipe down and washing the fryer basket in warm, soapy water. Excess fat, which might otherwise spatter or drip to the bottom of a conventional oven, is captured in the fryer and can simply be wiped away with a damp cloth.

It's convenient

The air fryer is compact enough to fit neatly on a countertop, and it takes up considerably less space than larger appliances that do much less. You can also use the air fryer for reheating food as well as restoring crunch to breaded foods that have lost their texture.

You can cook faster

Because superheated air circulates through the cooking chamber by convection, food takes less time to cook than if it was cooked in a conventional oven. Many air fryers also have built-in presets, so controlling the exact cook times and temperatures is simple.

Heated air circulates over all areas of the compartment

Bottom of the chamber forces hot air upward

Air Frying vs. Oil Frying

In addition to its versatility and convenience, one of the air fryer's great benefits is cooking food with significantly less oil, which means air-fried food is healthier and has fewer calories than foods cooked in other ways.

Air-fried French fries

You can turn two russet potatoes into a single serving of French fries that have fewer calories and less fat than traditional deep-fried French fries. You'll still taste that delicious potato flavor and enjoy a crisp, crunchy, golden brown texture, but you won't consume the excess fat or calories that come from deep frying.

204 CALORIES

5g FAT

Air-fried French fries contain as much as **70–80% less fat** than those sold at your local fast-food place.

No oil transfers to brown paper with air-fried foods!

500
CALORIES

24g
FAT

You could consume more fat than you realize with oil-fried foods!

Oil-fried French fries

A large serving of French fries deep fried in oil can contain more than twice as many calories and almost five times as much fat as air-fried French fries. This means that roughly 220 of the calories come from fat, which equates to almost 40% of your daily value of fat in one meal. That's nearly five times the amount of fat compared with a serving of air-fried French fries!

Healthier Options

Olive oil makes air frying easier, safer—and healthier!

Olive and canola oils: Some recipes in this book do call for added oil. In most cases, it's either olive or canola, which are high in heart-healthy monounsaturated fats. You won't find any vegetable oil in this book, which means you'll avoid unhealthy trans fats.

Butter and buttery spreads: Some recipes also call for small amounts of a buttery spread. Use one made with plant-based oils and without trans fats. It typically contains up to 60 percent less saturated (unhealthy) fat compared with butter and can help lower cholesterol and improve heart health. And used in moderation, butter can still be a part of a healthy diet, particularly for baked goods, where the flavor of real butter is desired.

Air Fryer Tips

One of the great things about air frying is how easy it is to cook all your favorite foods. However, learning a few tips and tricks will help your air-fried food come out perfect every time.

Use parchment paper to minimize cleanup.

Line the bottom of the fryer basket or the air fryer baking pan with parchment paper for easier cleanup. The parchment paper will catch a lot of the excess grease that might drip from more fatty foods, but it won't catch fire.

Preheat the air fryer before cooking.

Preheating the air fryer will help the food cook more evenly because the temperature and air flow will be at their optimum levels when you place the food in the fryer. This process takes 3 minutes (or less).

Keep your air fryer clean to extend its life.

For best results, use a slightly damp paper towel or cloth to wipe out the fryer basket and baking pan after each use. Cleaning your air fryer might require some extra effort for fattier foods like meats or fish as well as recipes with a batter or breading. For these instances, you can soak your accessories in warm soapy water.

Use a baking pan for breaded foods.

Air circulation within the air fryer can cause bits of breading and small pieces of food to come loose and fly around the chamber. To prevent breading from breaking loose, cook foods inside the baking pan. Using a baking pan will also keep foods from falling apart as well as prevent a mess inside the air fryer.

Drain excess fat to minimize smoke.

When fat drips away from foods like steak and chicken wings, it can burn and create smoke that can escape from the air fryer. If this occurs, pause the air fryer, carefully drain the fat from the fryer basket or wipe off any oily fat from the food with a paper towel, then promptly return the basket to the air fryer and resume cooking.

Shake the basket to prevent uneven frying.

If you're experiencing uneven frying, it's typically because of overcrowding in the fryer basket. For more even frying, pause the air fryer once or twice (or as instructed) during the cooking process to gently shake the fryer basket. This will help redistribute the food so it cooks more evenly and browns on all sides.

Accessories to Consider

Most recipes in this book use the air fryer basket that comes with the air fryer. Some use the baking pan instead; the grill pan is something you might prefer for some recipes.

Baking pan

This is a must-have accessory for making cakes, dips, and casseroles. A 6-inch round baking pan will also work for most recipes, but this square nonstick model has been made specifically for the air fryer.

Grill pan

You can use this nonstick accessory for searing and grilling meat, fish, and vegetables. Most models will attach in the same spot as the fryer basket. And you'll still be able to get those great grill marks!

ABOUT THE RECIPES

The recipes in this book were developed and tested using the Phillips HD9220 and HD9230 air fryer models. Check your food a little earlier than specified the first time you make a recipe to ensure you can account for any necessary future adjustments. Most recipes in this book include instructions for spraying the fryer basket or baking pan with nonstick cooking spray, which isn't included in the ingredients or nutritional data because the nutritional impact is negligible. Use a nonstick spray made from canola oil.

BREAK FAST ESSENTIALS

Your air fryer can cook almost anything you'd normally make for breakfast, but these recipes are healthier than traditional staples and ideal ways to start your day.

301 CALORIES
PER SERVING

MAKES **3 cups**
SERVING SIZE **1½ cups**
PREP TIME **10 minutes**
COOK TIME **10 minutes**
FRYER TEMP **300°F**

This take on a classic breakfast dish is part oatmeal, part pumpkin bread—and all delicious. This egg-free recipe lets you enjoy autumn flavors all year long.

Pumpkin Oatmeal

1 cup rolled oats

2 TB. raisins

¼ tsp. ground cinnamon

Pinch of kosher salt

¼ cup canned pumpkin puree

2 TB. maple syrup

1 cup low-fat milk

1. Preheat the air fryer to 300°F.

2. In a medium bowl, combine the rolled oats, raisins, ground cinnamon, and kosher salt, then stir in the pumpkin puree, maple syrup, and low-fat milk.

3. Spray the air fryer baking pan with nonstick cooking spray, then pour the oatmeal mixture into the pan and cook for 10 minutes.

4. Remove the oatmeal from the fryer and allow to cool in the pan on a wire rack for 5 minutes before serving.

NUTRITION PER SERVING

Total fat **4g**	Cholesterol **8mg**	Carbohydrates **57g**	Sugars **26g**
Saturated fat **1g**	Sodium **140mg**	Dietary fiber **6g**	Protein **10g**

Hearty steel-cut oats and sweet apples make for a comforting and satisfying breakfast combo—with plenty of carbs for energy in the morning.

Steel-Cut Oats with Fried Apples

183 CALORIES PER SERVING

MAKES **3 cups**
SERVING SIZE **1½ cups**
PREP TIME **10 minutes**
COOK TIME **40 minutes**
FRYER TEMP **390°F**

1 cup dry steel-cut oats

4 cups water

Pinch of kosher salt

1 large Gala apple, cored and cut into 10 slices

⅛ tsp. ground cinnamon

1 TB. granulated sugar

1. In a medium saucepan, combine the steel-cut oats, water, and kosher salt. Bring the mixture to a boil, reduce the heat to a simmer, and cook uncovered for 30 minutes or until the oats are tender. Set aside.

2. Preheat the air fryer to 390°F.

3. Spray the fryer basket with nonstick cooking spray, then place the apple slices in the basket and cook for 10 minutes.

4. While the apples cook, combine the ground cinnamon and granulated sugar in a small bowl and set aside.

5. Remove the apple slices from the fryer and place on a serving plate. Sprinkle 1 teaspoon of the cinnamon sugar mix on the apples. (Reserve the remainder for another use.)

6. Allow the apples to cool for 5 minutes, then serve on top of the cooked oats.

NUTRITION PER SERVING

Total fat **3g**	Cholesterol **0mg**	Carbohydrates **36g**	Sugars **8g**
Saturated fat **1g**	Sodium **36mg**	Dietary fiber **5g**	Protein **5g**

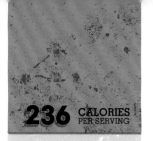

236 CALORIES PER SERVING

MAKES **6**
SERVING SIZE **1**
PREP TIME **10 minutes**
COOK TIME **12–14 minutes**
FRYER TEMP **390°F**

Yes, you *can* make baked goods in the air fryer! Packed with whole grains, these squares taste like they're fresh from a bakery.

Blueberry Oat Squares

1 cup all-purpose flour

1 cup quick-cook oats

¼ tsp. baking powder

Pinch of kosher salt

¼ tsp. ground cinnamon

1 large egg, beaten

¼ cup light brown sugar, packed

¼ cup unsweetened applesauce

¼ cup canola oil

¼ cup low-fat milk

1 cup fresh blueberries

1 tsp. confectioners' sugar

1. Preheat the air fryer to 390°F.

2. In a large bowl, whisk together the all-purpose flour, quick-cook oats, baking powder, kosher salt, and ground cinnamon. Set aside.

3. In a separate large bowl, combine the egg, light brown sugar, unsweetened applesauce, canola oil, and low-fat milk.

4. Add the egg mixture to the flour mixture, stirring until just combined, then gently fold in the blueberries.

5. Spray the air fryer baking pan with nonstick cooking spray, then pour the batter into the pan. Cook for 12–14 minutes or until golden brown and a toothpick comes out clean when inserted in the middle.

6. Remove the pan from the fryer and allow to cool on a wire rack for 10 minutes. Dust the confectioners' sugar on top before cutting and serving.

NUTRITION PER SERVING

Total fat **11g**	Cholesterol **31 mg**	Carbohydrates **32g**	Sugars **12g**
Saturated fat **1g**	Sodium **61mg**	Dietary fiber **2g**	Protein **4g**

277 CALORIES
PER SERVING

MAKES **1**
SERVING SIZE **1**
PREP TIME **10 minutes**
COOK TIME **15 minutes**
FRYER TEMP **360°F**

This high-protein burrito—bursting with flavor and nutritional value, especially from the black beans and whole grain tortilla—will kick-start your day.

Egg, Mushroom & Bean Burrito

2 TB. canned
  black beans,
  rinsed and drained

¼ cup baby portobello
  mushrooms, sliced

1 tsp. olive oil

Pinch of kosher salt

1 large egg

1 slice low-fat
  cheddar cheese

1 eight-inch whole grain
  flour tortilla

Hot sauce (optional)

1. Preheat the air fryer to 360°F.

2. Spray the air fryer baking pan with nonstick cooking spray, then place the black beans and baby portobello mushrooms in the pan, drizzle with the olive oil, and season with the kosher salt.

3. Cook for 5 minutes, then pause the fryer to crack the egg on top of the beans and mushrooms. Cook for 8 more minutes or until the egg is cooked as desired.

4. Pause the fryer again, top the egg with cheese, and cook for 1 more minute.

5. Remove the pan from the fryer, then use a spatula to place the bean mixture on the whole grain flour tortilla. Fold in the sides and roll from front to back. Serve warm with the hot sauce on the side (if using).

A similar version from a fast-food place usually has more than 500 calories!

NUTRITION PER SERVING

Total fat **12g**	Cholesterol **189mg**	Carbohydrates **26g**	Sugars **2g**
Saturated fat **5g**	Sodium **306mg**	Dietary fiber **6g**	Protein **16g**

Crispy kale, fluffy eggs (kept light by lowering the temperature during the cooking process), and creamy feta make this breakfast a morning home run.

Kale & Feta Frittatas

216 CALORIES PER SERVING

MAKES **2**
SERVING SIZE **1**
PREP TIME **5 minutes**
COOK TIME **11 minutes**
FRYER TEMP **360°F**

1 cup kale, chopped

1 tsp. olive oil

4 large eggs, beaten

2 TB. water

Pinch of kosher salt

3 TB. crumbled feta

1. Preheat the air fryer to 360°F.

2. Spray the air fryer baking pan with nonstick cooking spray, then place the kale in the pan, drizzle with the olive oil, and cook for 3 minutes.

3. While the kale cooks, whisk together the eggs, water, and kosher salt in a large bowl.

4. Pause the fryer to pour the eggs into the pan and sprinkle the feta on top. Reduce the heat to 300°F and cook for 8 more minutes.

5. Remove the frittatta from the fryer and allow to cool in the pan on a wire rack for 5 minutes before cutting and serving.

NUTRITION PER SERVING

Total fat **15g**	Cholesterol **385mg**	Carbohydrates **5g**	Sugars **2g**
Saturated fat **6g**	Sodium **354mg**	Dietary fiber **1g**	Protein **16g**

You can cook and enjoy these hearty egg sandwiches immediately or freeze them for later. And the Canadian bacon is a lower-fat alternative to traditional bacon.

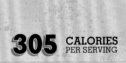

305 CALORIES PER SERVING

MAKES **2**
SERVING SIZE **1**
PREP TIME **3 minutes**
COOK TIME **8 minutes**
FRYER TEMP **360°F**

Bacon & Egg Sandwiches

2 large eggs

¼ tsp. kosher salt, divided

¼ tsp. freshly ground black pepper, divided (plus extra for serving)

2 slices Canadian bacon

2 slices American cheese

2 whole grain English muffins, sliced in half

1. Preheat the air fryer to 360°F.

2. Spray two 3-inch ramekins with nonstick cooking spray, then crack one egg into each ramekin and add half the kosher salt and half the black pepper to each egg.

3. Place the ramekins in the fryer basket and cook for 5 minutes.

4. Pause the fryer and top each partially cooked egg with a slice of Canadian bacon and a slice of American cheese.

5. Cook for 3 more minutes or until the cheese has melted and the egg yolk has just cooked through.

6. Remove the ramekins from the fryer and allow to cool on a wire rack for 2–3 minutes, then flip the eggs, bacon, and cheese out onto English muffins and sprinkle some black pepper on top before serving.

NUTRITION PER SERVING

Total fat **13g**	Cholesterol **216mg**	Carbohydrates **26g**	Sugars **3g**
Saturated fat **5g**	Sodium **618mg**	Dietary fiber **3g**	Protein **22g**

This recipe not only gives you something sweet to eat for breakfast, but it also provides plenty of protein—supplying almost half your daily needs.

Caramelized Banana Slices with Yogurt

1 banana, cut into ¾-inch slices

6 oz. nonfat plain Greek yogurt

3 TB. Toasted Granola with Almonds (see page 28)

1. Preheat the air fryer to 360°F.

2. Spray the fryer basket with nonstick cooking spray, then place the banana slices in the basket and cook for 5 minutes.

3. Allow to cool in the fryer for 5 minutes, then remove the banana slices from the fryer.

4. Spread the plain Greek yogurt on a serving plate, then place the banana slices on the yogurt and top with the toasted granola before serving.

NUTRITION PER SERVING

| Total fat **3g** | Cholesterol **0mg** | Carbohydrates **40g** | Sugars **23g** |
| Saturated fat **1g** | Sodium **96mg** | Dietary fiber **4g** | Protein **18g** |

You can still make French toast as part of a healthy breakfast by cutting back on the fat and boosting the fiber. Serve this lighter version with fresh fruit.

221 CALORIES
PER SERVING

MAKES **2 slices**
SERVING SIZE **1 slice**
PREP TIME **8 minutes**
COOK TIME **8 minutes**
FRYER TEMP **360°F**

Whole Grain French Toast

2 slices whole grain bread

1 large egg

½ cup low-fat milk

⅛ tsp. ground cinnamon

½ tsp. vanilla extract

2 tsp. maple syrup
(plus 2 TB. for serving)

1 tsp. confectioners'
sugar (for serving)

1. Preheat the air fryer to 360°F.

2. Spray the air fryer baking pan with nonstick cooking spray, then cut the whole grain bread into small pieces or strips and place in the pan. Set aside.

3. In a medium bowl, whisk together the egg, low-fat milk, ground cinnamon, vanilla extract, and 2 teaspoons of maple syrup.

4. Pour the egg mixture over the bread, then press it down with a spatula to make sure all the bread is coated and cook for 8 minutes.

5. Remove the French toast from the fryer and allow to cool in the pan on a wire rack for 5 minutes, then dust with the confectioners' sugar and drizzle 2 tablespoons of maple syrup on top before serving.

NUTRITION PER SERVING

| Total fat **4g** | Cholesterol **97mg** | Carbohydrates **37g** | Sugars **21g** |
| Saturated fat **1g** | Sodium **239mg** | Dietary fiber **2g** | Protein **9g** |

163 CALORIES
PER SERVING

MAKES 1⅓ cups
SERVING SIZE ⅓ cup
PREP TIME 5 minutes
COOK TIME 8-10 minutes
FRYER TEMP 360°F

Made-from-scratch granola needs only a few staple ingredients. For extra texture and flavor, add a handful of dried fruit after baking the granola.

Toasted Granola with Almonds

⅔ cup rolled oats

⅓ cup shredded sweetened coconut

⅓ cup sliced almonds

1 tsp. canola oil

2 tsp. honey

¼ tsp. kosher salt

1. Preheat the air fryer to 360°F.

2. In a medium bowl, combine the rolled oats, shredded sweetened coconut, sliced almonds, canola oil, honey, and kosher salt.

3. Place a small piece of parchment paper on the bottom of the air fryer baking pan, then pour the mixture into the pan and distribute it evenly. Cook for 5 minutes, pause the fryer to gently stir the granola, and cook for 3 more minutes.

4. Remove the granola from the fryer and allow to cool in the pan on a wire rack for 5 minutes, then transfer the granola to a serving plate to cool completely before serving. (It becomes crunchier as it cools. Store the granola in an airtight container for up to 2 weeks.)

NUTRITION PER SERVING

Total fat **9g**	Cholesterol **0mg**	Carbohydrates **18g**	Sugars **7g**
Saturated fat **3g**	Sodium **94mg**	Dietary fiber **3g**	Protein **4g**

185 CALORIES PER SERVING

MAKES **4 slices**
SERVING SIZE **1 slice**
PREP TIME **10 minutes**
COOK TIME **8 minutes**
FRYER TEMP **300°F**

Antioxidant-rich raspberries are underutilized in breads, but the subtle sweetness mixes beautifully with the tang of vanilla yogurt in this breakfast cake.

Raspberry Yogurt Cake

½ cup whole wheat pastry flour

⅛ tsp. kosher salt

¼ tsp. baking powder

½ cup whole milk vanilla yogurt

2 TB. canola oil

2 TB. maple syrup

¾ cup fresh raspberries

1 tsp. confectioners' sugar (for serving)

1. Preheat the air fryer to 300°F.

2. In a large bowl, combine the whole wheat pastry flour, kosher salt, and baking powder, then stir in the whole milk vanilla yogurt, canola oil, and maple syrup and gently fold in the raspberries.

3. Spray the air fryer baking pan with nonstick cooking spray, then pour the cake batter into the pan and cook for 8 minutes.

4. Remove the cake from the fryer and allow to cool in the pan on a wire rack for 10 minutes, then sift the confectioners' sugar on top before cutting and serving.

NUTRITION PER SERVING

Total fat **8g**	Cholesterol **4mg**	Carbohydrates **25g**	Sugars **12g**
Saturated fat **1g**	Sodium **82mg**	Dietary fiber **3g**	Protein **3g**

Enjoy this light breakfast on a busy weekday or during a lazy weekend, especially because it offers a protein boost in just 40 calories!

40 CALORIES PER SERVING

MAKES **1**
SERVING SIZE **1**
PREP TIME **5 minutes**
COOK TIME **10 minutes**
FRYER TEMP **300°F**

Spinach & Tomato Egg White Cup

2 egg whites, beaten

2 TB. tomato, chopped

2 TB. spinach, chopped

Pinch of kosher salt

Red pepper flakes (optional)

1. Preheat the air fryer to 300°F.

2. Spray a 3-inch ramekin with nonstick cooking spray, then combine the egg whites, tomato, spinach, kosher salt, and red pepper flakes (if using) in the ramekin.

3. Place the ramekin in the air fryer basket and cook for 10 minutes or until the eggs have set.

4. Remove the ramekin from the fryer and allow to cool on a wire rack for 5 minutes before serving.

NUTRITION PER SERVING

Total fat **0g**	Cholesterol **0mg**	Carbohydrates **1g**	Sugars **1g**
Saturated fat **0g**	Sodium **184mg**	Dietary fiber **1g**	Protein **7g**

These pretty egg cups have all the flavor of a diner omelet—but without any greasy butter or oil. Use this recipe for any combo of veggies and low-fat cheese.

176 CALORIES PER SERVING

MAKES **2**
SERVING SIZE **1**
PREP TIME **5 minutes**
COOK TIME **10 minutes**
FRYER TEMP **390°F**

Bell Pepper & Red Onion Omelet Cups

4 large eggs

½ bell pepper, finely chopped

1 TB. red onion, finely chopped

¼ tsp. kosher salt

¼ tsp. freshly ground black pepper (plus extra for serving)

2 TB. shredded cheddar cheese

1. Preheat the air fryer to 390°F.

2. In a large bowl, whisk together the eggs, then stir in the bell pepper, red onion, kosher salt, and black pepper.

3. Spray two 3-inch ramekins with nonstick cooking spray, then pour half the egg mixture into each ramekin and place the ramekins in the fryer basket. Cook for 8 minutes.

4. Pause the fryer, sprinkle 1 tablespoon of shredded cheddar cheese on top of each cup, and cook for 2 more minutes.

5. Remove the ramekins from the fryer and allow to cool on a wire rack for 5 minutes, then turn the omelet cups out on plates and sprinkle some black pepper on top before serving.

NUTRITION PER SERVING

Total fat **12g**	Cholesterol **378mg**	Carbohydrates **2g**	Sugars **1g**
Saturated fat **5g**	Sodium **333mg**	Dietary fiber **0g**	Protein **14g**

102 CALORIES
PER SERVING

MAKES **4 cups**
SERVING SIZE **1 cup**
PREP TIME **10 minutes**
COOK TIME **20 minutes**
FRYER TEMP **360°F**

Home fries are a diner favorite but are typically cooked in a vat of grease. This version lets the potatoes' flavor and nutrition come through—without all that fat.

Classic Home Fries

1 lb. small red potatoes, diced

2 tsp. olive oil

¼ cup yellow onion, finely chopped

¼ tsp. kosher salt

¼ tsp. freshly ground black pepper

1. Preheat the air fryer to 360°F.

2. In a medium bowl, toss the red potatoes and olive oil, then add the onion, kosher salt, and black pepper, tossing again to coat.

3. Spray the fryer basket with nonstick cooking spray, then place the mixture in the basket and cook for 20 minutes or until golden brown, pausing the fryer every 5 minutes to shake the basket.

4. Remove the fries from the fryer, place on a plate lined with a paper towel, and allow to cool for 5 minutes before serving.

NUTRITION PER SERVING

Total fat **2g**	Cholesterol **0mg**	Carbohydrates **19g**	Sugars **2g**
Saturated fat **0g**	Sodium **161mg**	Dietary fiber **2g**	Protein **2g**

Spice up your morning with this one-dish breakfast. This dish is a fantastic way to use up day-old bread, and it offers plenty of protein to start your day.

Ham & Egg Casserole

248 CALORIES PER SERVING

MAKES **2 halves**
SERVING SIZE **1 half**
PREP TIME **5 minutes**
COOK TIME **12 minutes**
FRYER TEMP **360°F**

1 cup day-old whole grain bread, cubed

3 large eggs, beaten

2 TB. water

⅛ tsp. kosher salt

1 oz. prosciutto, roughly chopped

1 oz. slice pepper jack cheese, roughly chopped

1 TB. fresh chives, chopped

1. Preheat the air fryer to 360°F.

2. Spray the air fryer baking pan with nonstick cooking spray, then place the bread cubes in the pan.

3. In a medium bowl, whisk together the eggs and water, then stir in the kosher salt, prosciutto, pepper jack cheese, and chives.

4. Pour the egg mixture over the bread cubes and cook for 10–12 minutes or until the eggs have set and the top is golden brown.

5. Remove the casserole from the fryer and allow to cool in the pan on a wire rack for 5 minutes before cutting and serving.

NUTRITION PER SERVING

Total fat **6g**	Cholesterol **299mg**	Carbohydrates **11g**	Sugars **2g**
Saturated fat **6g**	Sodium **557mg**	Dietary fiber **3g**	Protein **19g**

220 CALORIES
PER SERVING

MAKES **1**
SERVING SIZE **1**
PREP TIME **5 minutes**
COOK TIME **10 minutes**
FRYER TEMP **360°F**

Avocado toast has become a healthy breakfast trend. This version includes extra protein from an egg as well as extra nutrients from a tomato.

Egg-in-a-Hole with Avocado

1 slice whole grain bread

1 large egg

⅛ tsp. kosher salt

¼ cup avocado, diced

¼ cup tomato, diced

Pinch of freshly ground black pepper

1. Preheat the air fryer to 360°F.

2. Spray the air fryer baking pan with nonstick cooking spray, then use a ring mold or a sharp knife to cut a 3-inch hole in the center of the whole grain bread. Place the bread slice and the circle in the pan.

3. Crack the egg into the hole, then season with the kosher salt. Cook for 5–7 minutes or until the egg is cooked as desired.

4. Remove the pan from the fryer and allow to cool on a wire rack for 5 minutes before transferring the toast to a plate, then sprinkle the avocado, tomato, and black pepper on top before serving.

NUTRITION PER SERVING

Total fat **12g**	Cholesterol **186mg**	Carbohydrates **18g**	Sugars **4g**
Saturated fat **2g**	Sodium **406mg**	Dietary fiber **5g**	Protein **10g**

218 CALORIES
PER SERVING

MAKES **4**
SERVING SIZE **1**
PREP TIME **10 minutes**
COOK TIME **35 minutes**
FRYER TEMP **330°F**

Breakfast pockets from the freezer section are loaded with fat, sodium, and preservatives. You can make a homemade version that's tastier and better for you.

Egg & Cheese Pockets

1 large egg, beaten

Pinch of kosher salt

½ sheet puff pastry

1 slice cheddar cheese, divided into 4 pieces

1. Preheat the air fryer to 330°F with the air fryer baking pan in the basket.

2. Pour the egg into the pan, season with the kosher salt, and cook for 3 minutes. Pause the fryer, gently scramble the egg, and cook for 2 more minutes. Remove the egg from the fryer, keeping the fryer on, and set the egg aside to slightly cool.

3. Roll the puff pastry out flat and divide into 4 pieces.

4. Place a piece of cheddar cheese and ¼ of the egg on one side of a piece of pastry, fold the pastry over the egg and cheese, and use a fork to press the edges closed. Repeat this process with the remaining pieces.

5. Place 2 pockets in the fryer and cook for 15 minutes or until golden brown. Repeat this process with the other 2 pockets.

6. Remove the pockets from the fryer and allow to cool on a wire rack for 5 minutes before serving.

Save more than 100 calories from typical breakfast pockets.

NUTRITION PER SERVING

Total fat **15g**	Cholesterol **54mg**	Carbohydrates **14g**	Sugars **0g**
Saturated fat **5g**	Sodium **143mg**	Dietary fiber **0g**	Protein **6g**

Homemade corn tortillas are the secret to amazing "ranchers eggs." Cooking them in the air fryer will make them crispy and delicious—without all the fat.

142 CALORIES PER SERVING

MAKES **4 tortillas**
SERVING SIZE **1 tortilla**
PREP TIME **20 minutes**
COOK TIME **25 minutes**
FRYER TEMP **330°F/390°F**

Huevos Rancheros

4 large eggs

¼ tsp. kosher salt

¼ cup masa harina (corn flour)

1 tsp. olive oil

¼ cup warm water

½ cup salsa

¼ cup crumbled queso fresco or feta cheese

1. Preheat the air fryer to 330°F with the air fryer baking pan in the basket.

2. Crack the eggs into the pan, season with the kosher salt, and cook for 3 minutes. Pause the fryer, gently scramble the eggs, and cook for 2 more minutes. Remove the eggs from the fryer, keeping the fryer on, and set the eggs aside to slightly cool. (Clean the baking pan before making the tortillas.)

3. Preheat the air fryer to 390°F.

4. In a medium bowl, combine the masa harina, olive oil, and ¼ teaspoon of kosher salt by hand, then slowly pour in the water, stirring until a soft dough forms.

5. Divide the dough into 4 equal balls, then place each ball between 2 pieces of parchment paper and use a pie plate or a rolling pin to flatten the dough.

6. Spray the air fryer baking pan with nonstick cooking spray, then place one flattened tortilla in the pan and cook for 5 minutes. Repeat this process with the remaining tortillas.

7. Remove the tortillas from the fryer and place on a serving plate, then top each tortilla with the scrambled eggs, salsa, and cheese before serving.

Traditional huevos rancheros recipes can have more than 500 calories!

NUTRITION PER SERVING

Total fat **8g**	Cholesterol **194mg**	Carbohydrates **8g**	Sugars **2g**
Saturated fat **3g**	Sodium **333mg**	Dietary fiber **1g**	Protein **8g**

Made with nutrient-rich sweet potatoes and enhanced by some heat from a jalapeño pepper, this hash will taste better than any fast-food version you've eaten.

Sweet Potato & Jalapeño Hash

121 CALORIES
PER SERVING

MAKES **4 cups**
SERVING SIZE **1 cup**
PREP TIME **10 minutes**
COOK TIME **19–20 minutes**
FRYER TEMP **360°F**

2 large sweet potatoes

½ small red onion, cut into large chunks

1 green bell pepper, cut into large chunks

1 jalapeño pepper, seeded and sliced

½ tsp. kosher salt

¼ tsp. freshly ground black pepper (plus extra for serving)

1 tsp. olive oil

1 large egg, poached

1. Preheat the air fryer to 360°F.

2. Cook the sweet potatoes on high in the microwave until softened but not completely cooked (3–4 minutes), then set aside to cool for 10 minutes.

3. Remove the skins from the sweet potatoes, then cut the sweet potatoes into large chunks.

4. In a large bowl, combine the sweet potatoes, red onion, green bell pepper, jalapeño pepper, kosher salt, black pepper, and olive oil, tossing gently.

5. Spray the fryer basket with nonstick cooking spray, then pour the mixture into the basket and cook for 8 minutes.

6. Pause the fryer to shake the basket, then cook for 8 more minutes or until golden brown.

7. Remove the hash from the fryer, place on a plate lined with a paper towel, and allow to cool for 5 minutes, then add the poached egg, sprinkle black pepper on top, and serve.

NUTRITION PER SERVING

Total fat **3g**	Cholesterol **47mg**	Carbohydrates **22g**	Sugars **7g**
Saturated fat **1g**	Sodium **174mg**	Dietary fiber **4g**	Protein **4g**

65 CALORIES PER SERVING

MAKES **2 cups**
SERVING SIZE **½ cup**
PREP TIME **5 minutes**
COOK TIME **15 minutes**
FRYER TEMP **360°F**

Prepare this warm apple topping for serving with breakfast favorites like oatmeal, pancakes, or yogurt. You can even add leftovers to a smoothie.

Apple Compote

- 2 medium apples, peeled and diced
- ⅛ tsp. ground cinnamon
- 2 tsp. honey
- Juice of ½ lemon
- 2 TB. raisins
- ⅔ cup water

1. Preheat the air fryer to 360°F.
2. Spray the air fryer baking pan with nonstick cooking spray, then combine the apples, ground cinnamon, honey, lemon juice, raisins, and water in the pan. Cook for 12–15 minutes or until the apples are tender.
3. Remove the compote from the fryer and allow to cool in the pan on a wire rack for 5 minutes before serving.

NUTRITION PER SERVING

Total fat **0g**	Cholesterol **0mg**	Carbohydrates **17g**	Sugars **14g**
Saturated fat **0g**	Sodium **3mg**	Dietary fiber **1g**	Protein **0g**

Enjoy this Mexican spin on breakfast! The air fryer quickly melts the cheese and puffs the tortilla, making for a mouthwatering grab-and-go meal.

Bacon, Egg & Cheese Quesadilla

335 CALORIES PER SERVING

MAKES **1**
SERVING SIZE **1**
PREP TIME **5 minutes**
COOK TIME **5 minutes**
FRYER TEMP **360°F**

1 large egg

⅛ tsp. kosher salt

1 eight-inch whole wheat tortilla

¼ cup shredded cheddar cheese

1 slice cooked bacon, chopped

1. Preheat the air fryer to 360°F with the air fryer baking pan in the fryer basket.

2. Pour the egg into the pan and season with the kosher salt. Cook for 3 minutes, then pause the fryer, gently scramble the egg, and cook for 2 more minutes.

3. Remove the egg from the fryer, keeping the fryer on, and set the egg aside to slightly cool.

4. Spray the fryer basket with nonstick cooking spray, then layer the cooked egg, shredded cheddar cheese, and bacon on the tortilla. Fold in half, place in the basket, and cook for 5 minutes.

5. Remove the quesadilla from the fryer and allow to cool on a wire rack for 2–3 minutes before serving.

A fast-food breakfast quesadilla can have more than 500 calories!

NUTRITION PER SERVING

Total fat **19g**	Cholesterol **227mg**	Carbohydrates **25g**	Sugars **1g**
Saturated fat **9g**	Sodium **480mg**	Dietary fiber **2g**	Protein **19g**

HEALTHIER MAINS

You can use the air fryer to make virtually any main dish, including pizza, steak fajitas, and even fried chicken—all with fewer calories and less fat.

97 CALORIES
PER SERVING

MAKES **6**

SERVING SIZE **1**

PREP TIME **15 minutes**

COOK TIME **10 minutes**

FRYER TEMP **360°F**

Packing these low-calorie pockets with nutrient-rich kale and savory mushrooms and cheese means you'll never have to feel guilty about eating pizza again!

Veggie Pizza Pockets

6 oz. pizza dough
(see page 52)

½ cup kale,
finely chopped

½ cup baby portobello
mushrooms,
finely chopped

½ cup shredded
part-skim mozzarella

Olive oil

1. Preheat the air fryer to 360°F.

2. Split the pizza dough into six 1-ounce balls, then roll each ball into a small circle. Place an equal amount of kale, baby portobello mushrooms, and mozzarella on each circle.

3. Gently fold the dough over the filling to create a pocket, then use a fork to crimp the edges closed. Brush each pocket with a little olive oil, then use a knife to poke a small hole in the top for steam to escape.

4. Spray the fryer basket with nonstick cooking spray, then place 2–3 pockets in the basket and cook for 5 minutes or until golden brown. Repeat this process with the remaining pockets.

5. Remove the pockets from the fryer and allow to cool on a wire rack for 5–10 minutes.

NUTRITION PER SERVING

| Total fat **3g** | Cholesterol **5mg** | Carbohydrates **13g** | Sugars **1g** |
| Saturated fat **1g** | Sodium **134mg** | Dietary fiber **1g** | Protein **4g** |

Give this Italian classic a reboot! Using part-skim cheeses saves hundreds of calories, and a crunchy topping takes the place of layers of fried eggplant.

Eggplant Parmesan

246 CALORIES PER SERVING

MAKES **2 pieces**
SERVING SIZE **1 piece**
PREP TIME **15 minutes**
COOK TIME **12 minutes**
FRYER TEMP **330°F**

1 small eggplant, peeled and thinly sliced

½ cup marinara sauce (see page 98)

½ cup shredded part-skim mozzarella cheese

½ cup part-skim ricotta cheese

2 TB. panko breadcrumbs

1. Preheat the air fryer to 330°F.

2. Spray the air fryer baking pan with nonstick cooking spray, then place the eggplant, marinara sauce, and mozzarella and rocotta cheeses in layers, finishing with a cheese layer, then sprinkle the panko breadcrumbs on top. Cook for 12 minutes or until the cheeses melt and bubble.

3. Remove the eggplant parmesan from the fryer and allow to cool in the pan on a wire rack for 10 minutes before cutting and serving.

Restaurant eggplant parmesan can typically set you back more than 1,000 calories!

NUTRITION PER SERVING

Total fat **9g**	Cholesterol **30mg**	Carbohydrates **28g**	Sugars **16g**
Saturated fat **4g**	Sodium **467mg**	Dietary fiber **10g**	Protein **17g**

These loaded peppers look amazing and are equally delicious. On a busy weeknight, you can enjoy this satisfying and healthy meal in less than 20 minutes.

266 CALORIES
PER SERVING

MAKES **2**
SERVING SIZE **1**
PREP TIME **10 minutes**
COOK TIME **8–10 minutes**
FRYER TEMP **360°F**

Quinoa-Stuffed Peppers with Salsa

2 medium red
bell peppers

½ cup baby portobello
mushrooms, chopped

1 cup cooked quinoa

½ cup cannellini beans,
rinsed and drained

1 tsp. tomato paste

¼ cup low-sodium
chicken broth

1 tsp. fresh thyme leaves,
chopped

¼ cup salsa

¼ cup shredded
part-skim
mozzarella cheese

1. Preheat the air fryer to 360°F.

2. Lay the red bell peppers on their sides, cut off a side on each, and scoop out the seeds. Set aside.

3. In a large bowl, gently toss the baby portobello mushrooms, quinoa, cannellini beans, tomato paste, chicken broth, and thyme leaves.

4. Fill each pepper with the quinoa mixture, add the salsa, and sprinkle the mozzarella cheese on top.

5. Spray the fryer basket with nonstick cooking spray, then place the peppers in the basket and cook for 8–10 minutes or until the peppers are tender and the cheese melts.

6. Remove the peppers from the fryer and allow to cool on a wire rack for 10 minutes before serving.

NUTRITION PER SERVING

Total fat **5g**	Cholesterol **8mg**	Carbohydrates **41g**	Sugars **9g**
Saturated fat **2g**	Sodium **319mg**	Dietary fiber **9g**	Protein **15g**

MAKES **12**
SERVING SIZE **3**
PREP TIME **15 minutes**
COOK TIME **15 minutes**
FRYER TEMP **360°F**

You'll savor the tropical flavors in these crunchy shrimp, which have just a hint of spicy hot sauce kick and are perfectly paired with a fresh mango sauce.

Coconut Shrimp with Mango Salsa

1 cup panko breadcrumbs

½ cup shredded sweetened coconut

1 TB. olive oil

1 egg white, beaten

⅛ tsp. kosher salt

¼ cup cornstarch

12 large cooked shrimp, peeled and deveined

For the salsa:

1 cup diced mango

Juice of 1 lime

1 tsp. Sriracha hot sauce

¼ cup water

1. Preheat the air fryer to 360°F.

2. In a small bowl, combine the panko breadcrumbs, shredded sweetened coconut, and olive oil. Set aside.

3. In another small bowl, season the egg white with the kosher salt and whisk well. Set aside.

4. Place the cornstarch in a plastic bag, add the shrimp, and shake to coat. Shake off any excess, then dip in the egg white, followed by the coconut mixture.

5. Spray the fryer basket with nonstick cooking spray, then place 6 shrimp in the basket and cook for 5–6 minutes. Repeat this process with the remaining shrimp.

6. While the shrimp cook, make the salsa in a blender by combining the mango, lime juice, and Sriracha hot sauce, then add the water and blend until smooth.

7. Remove the shrimp from the fryer, place on a plate lined with a paper towel, and allow to cool for 5 minutes before serving with the salsa.

These shrimp have roughly ¼ fewer calories than restaurant shrimp.

NUTRITION PER SERVING

Total fat **4g**	Cholesterol **71mg**	Carbohydrates **14g**	Sugars **6g**
Saturated fat **1g**	Sodium **307mg**	Dietary fiber **1g**	Protein **10g**

You don't need to make a trip to a fancy restaurant for crab cakes. You can make this decadent seafood treat in the air fryer with less fat—and fewer calories.

Lemon & Basil Crab Cakes

85 CALORIES PER SERVING

MAKES **4**
SERVING SIZE **1**
PREP TIME **10 minutes**
COOK TIME **20 minutes**
FRYER TEMP **360°F**

8 oz. jumbo lump crabmeat

1 slice multigrain bread, torn into pieces

2 TB. low-fat milk

1 large egg, beaten

2 TB. grated yellow onion

1 tsp. Dijon mustard

1 tsp. lemon zest

2 TB. basil, chopped

¼ tsp. kosher salt

¼ tsp. freshly ground black pepper

Lemon wedges (for serving)

1. Preheat the air fryer to 360°F.

2. Place the crabmeat in a small bowl to check for any shell pieces.

3. In a medium bowl, use a fork to combine the multigrain bread, low-fat milk, egg, onion, Dijon mustard, lemon zest, basil, kosher salt, black pepper, and crabmeat. Form the crab mixture into 4 cakes and spray each with nonstick cooking spray.

4. Spray the fryer basket with nonstick cooking spray, then place 2 cakes in the basket and cook for 5–8 minutes or until golden brown. Repeat this process with the remaining cakes.

5. Remove the crab cakes from the fryer and place on a wire rack. Serve warm with the lemon wedges.

NUTRITION PER SERVING

Total fat **3g**	Cholesterol **97mg**	Carbohydrates **5g**	Sugars **1g**
Saturated fat **0g**	Sodium **256mg**	Dietary fiber **1g**	Protein **11g**

244 CALORIES PER SERVING

MAKES **1**
SERVING SIZE **1**
PREP TIME **80 minutes**
COOK TIME **9–10 minutes**
FRYER TEMP **390°F**

For the dough:

1 tsp. dry active yeast

½ tsp. honey

½ cup warm water

1½ cups all-purpose flour

¼ tsp. kosher salt

1 tsp. olive oil

For the sauce:

1 TB. olive oil

1 garlic clove, minced

1 (28 oz.) can crushed tomatoes

½ tsp. kosher salt

For the pizza:

2 oz. pizza dough

1 TB. sauce

1 slice provolone cheese, torn into pieces

1 TB. shredded part-skim mozzarella cheese

Forget about pizza delivery! Make a homemade personal pan pizza in the air fryer with simple and fresh ingredients—and save on calories.

Deep-Dish Pizza

1. In a small bowl, whisk together the dry active yeast, honey, and water. Allow to rest for 10 minutes or until foamy.

2. While the yeast activates, make the dough in a large bowl by combining the all-purpose flour, kosher salt, and olive oil, then slowly pour in the yeast mixture. Combine with your hands until the dough forms a ball. (If it feels too dry, add more room temperature water 1 tablespoon at a time.)

3. Knead the dough in the bowl for 2–3 minutes or until smooth and elastic. Cover the bowl with a clean dish towel and allow the dough to rise for 1 hour.

4. While the dough rises, make the sauce by heating the olive oil in a medium saucepan. Add the minced garlic to the pan and sauté for 1 minute, then stir in the kosher salt and tomatoes, simmering for 20 more minutes.

5. Preheat the air fryer to 390°F.

6. Spray the air fryer baking pan with nonstick cooking spray, then divide the dough into six 2-ounce balls and press one ball into the pan, spreading it into every edge. (Wrap the remaining 5 balls of dough in freezer wrap or parchment paper.)

7. Spread 1 tablespoon of sauce evenly over the dough, then top with the provolone and mozzarella cheeses. (Refrigerate the remaining sauce in an airtight container.)

8. Cook for 9–10 minutes or until the crust is golden brown and the cheeses melt.

9. Remove the pizza from the fryer and allow to cool in the pan on a wire rack for 5 minutes before slicing and serving.

NUTRITION PER SERVING

Total fat **10g**	Cholesterol **23mg**	Carbohydrates **27g**	Sugars **2g**
Saturated fat **6g**	Sodium **445mg**	Dietary fiber **1g**	Protein **12g**

260 CALORIES
PER SERVING

MAKES **16**
SERVING SIZE **4**
PREP TIME **10 minutes**
COOK TIME **25 minutes**
FRYER TEMP **360°F**

Enjoy this Italian comfort food without a greasy mess!
This recipe makes incredible meatballs you can dunk
in a simple and healthy marinara sauce.

Zesty Meatballs with Marinara

1 lb. lean ground
sirloin beef
(90% lean
recommended)

2 TB. seasoned
breadcrumbs

1 large egg, beaten

¼ tsp. kosher salt

1 cup marinara sauce
(for serving)
(see page 98)

1. Preheat the air fryer to 360°F.

2. In a medium bowl, combine the ground beef,
seasoned breadcrumbs, egg, and kosher salt,
then form the mixture into sixteen 1-ounce balls.

3. Spray the fryer basket with nonstick cooking spray,
then place 5–6 balls in the basket and cook
for 8 minutes or until the internal temperature reaches
160°F. Repeat this process with the remaining balls.

4. Remove the meatballs from the fryer, place on a plate
lined with a paper towel, and allow to cool for 5 minutes
before serving with the marinara sauce for dipping.

NUTRITION PER SERVING

Total fat **14g**	Cholesterol **120mg**	Carbohydrates **7g**	Sugars **3g**
Saturated fat **5g**	Sodium **284mg**	Dietary fiber **1g**	Protein **25g**

These perfectly portioned sliders will satisfy any burger craving. Cook the meat ahead of time, rewarm in the air fryer, and serve with all your favorite fixings.

Game Day Sliders

209 CALORIES PER SERVING

MAKES **6**
SERVING SIZE **1**
PREP TIME **10 minutes**
COOK TIME **30 minutes**
FRYER TEMP **360°F**

1 lb. lean ground sirloin beef (90% lean recommended)

½ tsp. kosher salt

Pinch of freshly ground black pepper

6 whole wheat dinner rolls, sliced

1. Preheat the air fryer to 360°F.

2. Form the ground beef into 6 patties and season with the kosher salt and black pepper.

3. Spray the fryer basket with nonstick cooking spray, then place 2 burgers in the basket and cook for 8 minutes or until cooked as desired. Repeat this process with the remaining burgers.

4. Remove the burgers from the fryer, place on a plate lined with a paper towel, and allow to cool for 5–10 minutes. Place the burgers on the whole wheat dinner rolls and top as desired before serving.

Save 75 more calories by serving the burgers in lettuce wraps.

NUTRITION PER SERVING

| Total fat **9g** | Cholesterol **49mg** | Carbohydrates **13g** | Sugars **0g** |
| Saturated fat **3g** | Sodium **290mg** | Dietary fiber **1g** | Protein **18g** |

Craving soul food but prefer to not eat a day's worth of calories in one meal? Then this is the perfect recipe for you—healthier but still finger-licking good!

487 CALORIES PER SERVING

MAKES **4 thighs & 2 waffles**
SERVING SIZE
1 thigh & ¼ waffle
PREP TIME **90 minutes**
COOK TIME **40 minutes**
FRYER TEMP **360°F**

Lightened-Up Chicken & Waffles

For the chicken:

4 chicken thighs, skin on

1 cup low-fat buttermilk

½ cup all-purpose flour

1 tsp. kosher salt

½ tsp. freshly ground black pepper

½ tsp. mustard powder

½ tsp. garlic powder

¼ cup honey (for serving)

For the waffles:

½ cup whole wheat pastry flour

½ cup all-purpose flour

1 tsp. baking powder

½ tsp. kosher salt

1 TB. granulated sugar

2 TB. canola oil

1 cup low-fat buttermilk

1 large egg, beaten

1. Place the chicken thighs and buttermilk in a sealable plastic bag, then place the bag in the fridge to marinate for 1 hour or for up to 24 hours.

2. Preheat the air fryer to 360°F.

3. In a shallow dish, combine the all-purpose flour, kosher salt, black pepper, mustard powder, and garlic powder.

4. Remove the thighs from the buttermilk and pat dry with a paper towel. Dredge in the flour mixture, then the buttermilk, and finally the flour mixture again. Shake off any excess.

5. Spray the fryer basket with nonstick cooking spray, then place 2 thighs in the basket. Spray with a light coating of nonstick cooking spray, then cook for 20 minutes or until the internal temperature reaches 160°F. Repeat this process with the remaining thighs.

6. While the thighs cook, make the waffles in a large bowl by combining the whole wheat pastry flour, all-purpose flour, baking powder, kosher salt, granulated sugar, canola oil, low-fat buttermilk, and egg. (This makes 2 waffles. Freeze the leftover waffle for up to 3 months.) Use a waffle iron to cook each waffle until golden brown. Cut one waffle into 4 pieces.

7. Remove the thighs from the fryer and allow to cool on a wire rack for 15 minutes.

8. Place a chicken thigh on each warm waffle piece, then drizzle 1 tablespoon of honey on top before serving.

NUTRITION PER SERVING

Total fat **26g**	Cholesterol **160mg**	Carbohydrates **38g**	Sugars **21g**
Saturated fat **6g**	Sodium **528mg**	Dietary fiber **1g**	Protein **26g**

138 CALORIES PER SERVING

MAKES **8 skewers**
SERVING SIZE **2 skewers**
PREP TIME **30 minutes**
COOK TIME **5–7 minutes**
FRYER TEMP **360°F**

You can indeed enjoy a healthy steak thanks to the air fryer. A decadent sauce adds flavor and nutrition. Serve this meal with steamed veggies and brown rice.

Beef Satay with Peanut Sauce

4 bamboo skewers, cut in half

8 oz. London broil, sliced into 8 strips

2 tsp. curry powder

½ tsp. kosher salt

For the sauce:

2 TB. creamy peanut butter

1 TB. reduced-sodium soy sauce

2 tsp. rice vinegar

1 tsp. honey

1 tsp. grated ginger

1. Preheat the air fryer to 360°F.

2. Soak the bamboo skewers in room temperature water for 20 minutes before using to prevent them from burning in the air fryer. Set aside.

3. Season the London broil with curry powder and kosher salt, then thread the beef onto the skewers.

4. Spray the basket with nonstick cooking spray, then place the skewers in the basket and cook for 5–7 minutes or until the beef is cooked as desired.

5. While the beef cooks, make the sauce in a medium bowl by whisking together the peanut butter, soy sauce, rice vinegar, honey, and ginger.

6. Remove the beef from the fryer and allow to cool slightly in the pan on a wire rack before serving with the dipping sauce on the side.

NUTRITION PER SERVING

Total fat **7g**	Cholesterol **35mg**	Carbohydrates **4g**	Sugars **3g**
Saturated fat **2g**	Sodium **413mg**	Dietary fiber **1g**	Protein **14g**

You don't need to be a sports fan to love this game day favorite! Removing the oil from this recipe means this version has less fat and fewer calories.

Classic Buffalo Wings

147 CALORIES PER SERVING

MAKES **16**
SERVING SIZE **4**
PREP TIME **5 minutes**
COOK TIME **30 minutes**
FRYER TEMP **360°F**

16 chicken wings and drumettes

3 TB. hot sauce

1. Preheat the air fryer to 360°F.

2. Spray the fryer basket with nonstick cooking spray, then place 8 chicken wings in the basket and cook for 15 minutes, turning halfway through. Repeat this process with the remaining chicken wings.

3. Remove the wings from the fryer and place in a large bowl, then add the buffalo sauce and toss to coat. Transfer the wings to a serving plate. Serve warm.

Skip the blue cheese dip—it adds more than 75 calories and 8 grams of fat per tablespoon!

NUTRITION PER SERVING

Total fat **4g**	Cholesterol **66mg**	Carbohydrates **0g**	Sugars **0g**
Saturated fat **1g**	Sodium **350mg**	Dietary fiber **0g**	Protein **26g**

316 CALORIES
PER SERVING

MAKES **4**
SERVING SIZE **2**
PREP TIME **20 minutes**
COOK TIME **15 minutes**
FRYER TEMP **390°F**

Fiesta time! You can put everything needed for fajitas into the air fryer all at once for a healthy meal that's ready in less than 20 minutes.

Steak Fajitas & Corn Tortillas

8 oz. flank steak, sliced

¼ tsp. ground cumin

¼ tsp. kosher salt

¼ tsp. chili powder

1 red onion, sliced

1 green bell pepper, sliced

¼ cup tomato, chopped

2 TB. fresh cilantro, chopped

Squeeze of lime juice

4 six-inch corn tortillas

1. Preheat the air fryer to 390°F.

2. Place the steak in a large bowl, then add the cumin, kosher salt, and chili powder, tossing to coat.

3. Spray the fryer basket with nonstick cooking spray, then place the red onion and green bell pepper in the basket, place the meat on top, and cook for 15 minutes.

4. Remove the fajita mixture from the fryer, place on a serving plate, and allow to cool for 5–10 minutes. Serve on corn tortillas, then top with the tomato, cilantro, and a squeeze of lime juice.

Save 50 calories per serving by not using the corn tortillas.

NUTRITION PER SERVING

Total fat **8g**	Cholesterol **70mg**	Carbohydrates **33g**	Sugars **4g**
Saturated fat **3g**	Sodium **357mg**	Dietary fiber **5g**	Protein **29g**

MAKES **12**

SERVING SIZE **3**

PREP TIME **20 minutes**

COOK TIME **30 minutes**

FRYER TEMP **360°F**

These deliciously crispy and flavorful chicken fingers are perfect as toppers for salads, as event appetizers, or as kid-friendly dinners.

Chicken Fingers

½ cup all-purpose flour

2 cups panko breadcrumbs

1 large egg, beaten

2 TB. canola oil

Kosher salt

Freshly ground black pepper

3 boneless and skinless chicken breasts, each cut into 4 strips

1. Preheat the air fryer to 360°F.

2. Place the all-purpose flour, panko breadcrumbs, and egg into 3 separate shallow bowls, then season each bowl with a pinch of kosher salt and a pinch of black pepper. Stir the canola oil into the breadcrumbs.

3. Dredge the chicken strips in the flour, then the egg, and finally the breadcrumbs. Shake off any excess.

4. Spray the fryer basket with nonstick cooking spray, then place 4 chicken strips in the basket and cook for 10 minutes or until crispy and golden brown. Repeat this process with the remaining strips.

5. Remove the chicken strips from the fryer and allow to cool on a wire rack for 5 minutes. Season with a pinch of kosher salt before serving.

A fast-food order of chicken tenders has more than 600 calories per serving!

NUTRITION PER SERVING

Total fat **11g**	Cholesterol **176mg**	Carbohydrates **17g**	Sugars **1g**
Saturated fat **2g**	Sodium **285mg**	Dietary fiber **1g**	Protein **43g**

Double-coating this chicken is a messy job but totally worth the effort. The extra crispy and juicy result will amaze your taste buds!

Classic Fried Chicken

312 CALORIES PER SERVING

MAKES **8 pieces**
SERVING SIZE **2 pieces**
PREP TIME **90 minutes**
COOK TIME **40 minutes**
FRYER TEMP **360°F**

8 (24 oz.) bone-in chicken pieces

1 cup low-fat buttermilk

½ cup all-purpose flour

1 tsp. kosher salt

½ tsp. freshly ground black pepper

½ tsp. mustard powder

½ tsp. garlic powder

1. In a large bowl, place the chicken pieces and low-fat buttermilk, then cover the bowl with plastic wrap and marinate for 1 hour or for up to 24 hours.

2. Preheat the air fryer to 360°F.

3. In a shallow dish, combine the all-purpose flour, kosher salt, black pepper, mustard powder, and garlic powder.

4. Remove the chicken from the buttermilk and pat dry with a paper towel. Dredge the pieces in the flour mixture, then the buttermilk, and finally the flour again. Shake off any excess.

5. Spray the fryer basket with nonstick cooking spray, then place 4 pieces in the basket, spray with a light coating of cooking spray, and cook for 20 minutes or until the internal temperature reaches 160°F. Repeat this process with the remaining pieces.

6. Remove the chicken from the fryer and allow to cool on a wire rack for 10 minutes before serving.

NUTRITION PER SERVING

Total fat **20g**	Cholesterol **163mg**	Carbohydrates **4g**	Sugars **1g**
Saturated fat **6g**	Sodium **334mg**	Dietary fiber **0g**	Protein **30g**

Loaded with health-boosting omega-3 fatty acids, salmon lives up to all its nutrition hype. And in just 20 minutes, you can enjoy salmon with a tangy kick.

295 CALORIES PER SERVING

MAKES **2 pieces**
SERVING SIZE **1 piece**
PREP TIME **15 minutes**
COOK TIME **21 minutes**
FRYER TEMP **360°F**

Sweet & Sour Salmon

¼ cup orange juice (preferably freshly squeezed)

1 TB. reduced-sodium soy sauce

1 TB. ketchup

1 tsp. rice vinegar

1 tsp. honey

1 tsp. cornstarch

2 salmon steaks (5 oz. each), skin on

Pinch of kosher salt

Pinch of freshly ground black pepper

1. Preheat the air fryer to 360°F.

2. In a medium microwave-safe bowl, whisk together the orange juice, soy sauce, ketchup, rice vinegar, honey, and cornstarch. Cook in the microwave on high for 1 minute, then stir. (The sauce will thicken.) Reserve half the sauce in a small bowl and set aside.

3. Spray the fryer basket with nonstick cooking spray, then season the salmon with the kosher salt and black pepper, place the salmon (skin side down) in the basket, and cook for 5 minutes.

4. Pause the fryer to brush the salmon with half the sauce—don't flip the salmon—and cook for 5 more minutes. Repeat this process with the other steak.

5. Remove the salmon from the fryer, place on a serving plate, and serve warm with the reserved sauce on the side for dipping.

NUTRITION PER SERVING

| Total fat **15g** | Cholesterol **71mg** | Carbohydrates **10g** | Sugars **8g** |
| Saturated fat **4g** | Sodium **377mg** | Dietary fiber **0g** | Protein **28g** |

150 CALORIES
PER SERVING

MAKES **1 fillet**
SERVING SIZE **1 fillet**
PREP TIME **5 minutes**
COOK TIME **10 minutes**
FRYER TEMP **360°F**

Preparing fish is less intimidating with the air fryer. Cod is firm, mild, and quick cooking. When you season it with a few simple elements, the flavor explodes.

Roasted Cod with Sesame Seeds

1 TB. reduced-sodium
soy sauce

2 tsp. honey

1 tsp. sesame seeds

6 oz. fresh cod fillet

1. Preheat the air fryer to 360°F.

2. In a small bowl, combine the soy sauce and honey.

3. Spray the fryer basket with nonstick cooking spray, then place the cod in the basket, brush with the soy mixture, and sprinkle sesame seeds on top. Cook for 7–9 minutes or until opaque.

4. Remove the fish from the fryer and allow to cool on a wire rack for 5 minutes before serving.

NUTRITION PER SERVING

| Total fat **1g** | Cholesterol **80mg** | Carbohydrates **7g** | Sugars **6g** |
| Saturated fat **0g** | Sodium **466mg** | Dietary fiber **1g** | Protein **26g** |

You won't believe how simple it is to make this elegant shrimp dish with the air fryer. Your kitchen will smell like lemon and garlic in a matter of minutes.

Shrimp Scampi

333 CALORIES PER SERVING

MAKES **30 shrimp**
SERVING SIZE **15 shrimp**
PREP TIME **10 minutes**
COOK TIME **10 minutes**
FRYER TEMP **360°F**

30 (1 lb.) uncooked large shrimp, peeled, deveined, and tails removed

2 tsp. olive oil

1 garlic clove, thinly sliced

Juice and zest of ½ lemon

⅛ tsp. kosher salt

Pinch of red pepper flakes (optional)

1 TB. fresh parsley, chopped

1. Preheat the air fryer to 360°F.

2. Spray the air fryer baking pan with nonstick cooking spray, then combine the shrimp, olive oil, sliced garlic, lemon juice and zest, kosher salt, and red pepper flakes (if using) in the pan, tossing to coat. Cook for 7–8 minutes or until firm and bright pink.

3. Remove the shrimp from the fryer, place on a serving plate, and sprinkle the parsley on top. Serve warm.

NUTRITION PER SERVING

| Total fat **13g** | Cholesterol **340mg** | Carbohydrates **5g** | Sugars **1g** |
| Saturated fat **1g** | Sodium **383mg** | Dietary fiber **0g** | Protein **46g** |

MAKES **20**

SERVING SIZE **4**

PREP TIME **15 minutes**

COOK TIME **20 minutes**

FRYER TEMP **390°F**

This air fryer take on an Asian classic is a fabulous way to repurpose leftover chicken. Use a box grater to grate the veggies for a more delicate texture.

BBQ Wontons

2 TB. carrots, grated

2 TB. zucchini, grated

¼ cup skinless chicken, cooked and finely diced

1 TB. pickled jalapeños, finely chopped

3 TB. cream cheese, softened

2 tsp. BBQ sauce

20 wonton wrappers

1 TB. canola oil

1. Preheat the air fryer to 390°F.

2. Wrap the grated carrots and zucchini in a paper towel and squeeze out any excess liquid.

3. In a large bowl, combine the carrots, zucchini, chicken, jalapeños, cream cheese, and BBQ sauce.

4. Place a tablespoon of the filling in the center of a wonton wrapper. Apply a small amount of water along the edges of the wrapper to help seal it, then fold to form a triangle. (If the wrappers are coated with flour, place the filling on the floured side.)

5. Repeat this process with the remaining wontons and place on a plate, covering with a damp paper towel. Before cooking, brush each with a little canola oil.

6. Spray the air fryer baking pan with nonstick cooking spray, then place 5 wontons in the pan and cook for 4 minutes or until golden brown. Repeat this process with the remaining wontons.

7. Remove the wontons from the fryer and allow to cool on a wire rack for 5 minutes before serving.

Traditional fried wontons can easily top 500 calories— for an appetizer!

NUTRITION PER SERVING

Total fat **6g**	Cholesterol **19mg**	Carbohydrates **21g**	Sugars **1g**
Saturated fat **2g**	Sodium **288mg**	Dietary fiber **1g**	Protein **6g**

84 CALORIES
PER SERVING

MAKES **4**
SERVING SIZE **1**
PREP TIME **15 minutes**
COOK TIME **15 minutes**
FRYER TEMP **360°F**

These savory spring rolls are a lighter and tastier alternative to traditional deep-fried spring rolls, which can be loaded with deep-fried calories and fat.

Vegetable Spring Rolls

1 TB. olive oil, divided

2 cups shredded cabbage

1 cup baby portobello mushrooms, chopped

1 tsp. reduced-sodium soy sauce

4 egg roll wrappers

1. Preheat the air fryer to 360°F.

2. Place 1 teaspoon of olive oil in a small skillet and heat on medium-high, then add the cabbage, baby portobello mushrooms, and soy sauce. Sauté for 2 minutes.

3. Place 2 tablespoons of filling in the center of an egg roll wrapper. Apply a small amount of water along the edges to help seal the wrapper, then fold in the sides and roll lengthwise. Repeat this process with the remaining wrappers, then brush the wrappers with the remaining 2 teaspoons of olive oil.

4. Spray the fryer basket with nonstick cooking spray, then place 2 rolls in the basket and cook for 5–7 minutes or until golden brown. Repeat this process with the remaining rolls.

5. Remove the spring rolls from the fryer and allow to cool on a wire rack for 5 minutes before serving.

NUTRITION PER SERVING

Total fat **3g**	Cholesterol **3mg**	Carbohydrates **13g**	Sugars **1g**
Saturated fat **0g**	Sodium **121mg**	Dietary fiber **1g**	Protein **3g**

Roasted pork tucked into a flaky pastry will take you to empanada heaven. Add some kale, spinach, or other favorite veggies to boost nutrients—but not calories.

308 CALORIES
PER SERVING

MAKES **8**
SERVING SIZE **2**
PREP TIME **20 minutes**
COOK TIME **35–40 minutes**
FRYER TEMP **360°F/390°F**

Spicy Pork Empanadas

6 oz. pork tenderloin

Kosher salt

Freshly ground
black pepper

2 TB. spicy BBQ sauce

8 oz. prepared pie crust

1. Preheat the air fryer to 360°F.

2. Spray the fryer basket with nonstick cooking spray and season the pork with the kosher salt and black pepper, then place the pork in the basket. Cook for 20 minutes or until the internal temperature reaches 145°F.

3. Remove from the fryer and allow to cool on a wire rack for 10 minutes. (Clean the basket while the pork cools.)

4. Preheat the fryer temperature to 390°F.

5. Once the pork has cooled, finely shred it, then combine the pork and BBQ sauce in a medium bowl.

6. Roll out the pie crust and cut out eight 4-inch-diameter circles, then place individual tablespoons of pork in the center of each piece. Gently fold the dough over, creating a pocket, and use a fork to crimp the edges closed and a knife to poke a small hole in the top of each empanada to allow steam to escape.

7. Spray the fryer basket with nonstick cooking spray, then place 2–3 empanadas in the basket and cook for 5 minutes or until golden brown. Repeat this process with the remaining empanadas.

8. Remove the empanadas from the fryer and allow to cool on a wire rack for 5 minutes before serving.

NUTRITION PER SERVING

Total fat **13g**	Cholesterol **20mg**	Carbohydrates **31g**	Sugars **5g**
Saturated fat **5g**	Sodium **334mg**	Dietary fiber **0g**	Protein **12g**

354 CALORIES PER SERVING

MAKES **4 cups**
SERVING SIZE **2 cups**
PREP TIME **15 minutes**
COOK TIME **20 minutes**
FRYER TEMP **390°F**

Don't think you like tofu? You've never had it fried! Cooking tofu in an air fryer creates a crunchy crust, making this plant-based protein irresistible.

Fried Tofu with Stir-Fry Vegetables

8 oz. extra-firm tofu, cubed

2 tsp. canola oil

¼ tsp. kosher salt

2 cups sugar snap peas

1 bell pepper, thinly sliced

2 tsp. reduced-sodium soy sauce

1½ cups brown rice, cooked

1. Preheat the air fryer to 390°F.

2. Spray the fryer basket with nonstick cooking spray, then pat the tofu dry with a paper towel, place in the basket, drizzle the canola oil on top, and cook for 12 minutes or until golden brown and crispy.

3. Remove the tofu from the fryer and place on a plate lined with a paper towel, then sprinkle the kosher salt on top. Set aside to cool slightly. (Clean the basket before cooking the vegetables.)

4. Spray the fryer basket with nonstick cooking spray, then add the sugar snap peas, bell pepper, and soy sauce to the basket and cook for 5 minutes.

5. Remove the peas and pepper slices from the fryer, then place half the cooked rice on a serving plate and add half the tofu, peas, and pepper slices. Serve warm.

NUTRITION PER SERVING

| Total fat **11g** | Cholesterol **0mg** | Carbohydrates **48g** | Sugars **8g** |
| Saturated fat **1g** | Sodium **277mg** | Dietary fiber **7g** | Protein **20g** |

Make this scrumptious panini in less than 5 minutes, stacked with lean turkey breast, tangy peppers, zesty Dijon mustard—and without all the grease.

Red Pepper & Turkey Panini

2 slices whole grain bread

2 tsp. Dijon mustard

2 slices low-fat Swiss cheese

2 oz. thinly sliced cooked turkey breast

3 strips roasted red pepper

1. Preheat the air fryer to 330°F.

2. Spread one side of both slices of whole grain bread with Dijon mustard. Assemble the panini by layering the Swiss cheese, turkey, and roasted red pepper in your preferred order between the bread slices, then lightly spray the outer sides of the bread with nonstick cooking spray.

3. Spray the fryer basket with nonstick cooking spray, then place the sandwich in the basket and cook for 5 minutes or until the bread is toasted and the cheese melts.

4. Remove the panini from the fryer, place on a wire rack, and serve warm.

A typical restaurant panini has more than 500 calories!

NUTRITION PER SERVING

Total fat **5g**	Cholesterol **40mg**	Carbohydrates **38g**	Sugars **7g**
Saturated fat **1g**	Sodium **879mg**	Dietary fiber **3g**	Protein **29g**

Looking for a way to perk up your lunchtime routine? You'll never feel the same about a ham sandwich after experiencing this warm and toasty panini.

Ultimate Ham & Cheese Panini

320 CALORIES PER SERVING

MAKES **1**
SERVING SIZE **1**
PREP TIME **5 minutes**
COOK TIME **5 minutes**
FRYER TEMP **300°F**

2 slices whole grain bread

2 tsp. Dijon mustard

2 thin slices low-fat cheddar cheese

1 oz. thinly sliced cooked low-sodium ham

3 thin slices Granny Smith apple

1. Preheat the air fryer to 300°F.

2. Spread one side of both slices of whole grain bread with Dijon mustard. Assemble the panini by layering the cheddar cheese, ham, and apple slices in your preferred order between the bread slices, then lightly spray the outer sides of the bread with nonstick cooking spray.

3. Spray the fryer basket with nonstick cooking spray, then place the sandwich in the basket and cook for 5 minutes or until the bread is toasted and the cheese melts.

4. Remove the panini from the fryer, place on a wire rack, and serve warm.

NUTRITION PER SERVING

Total fat **6g**	Cholesterol **18mg**	Carbohydrates **45g**	Sugars **12g**
Saturated fat **1g**	Sodium **708mg**	Dietary fiber **7g**	Protein **21g**

Tex-Mex food doesn't have to feel heavy or be high in calories. And nothing is more Tex-Mex than tacos and salsa—all made easier with the air fryer.

Fish Tacos with Avocado Salsa

455 CALORIES PER SERVING

MAKES **8**
SERVING SIZE **2**
PREP TIME **20 minutes**
COOK TIME **40 minutes**
FRYER TEMP **390°F**

½ cup all-purpose flour

1 large egg, beaten

2 cups panko
  breadcrumbs

¾ tsp. kosher salt

¾ freshly ground
  black pepper

1 lb. cod, cut into
  16 strips

2 TB. canola oil

8 six-inch corn tortillas

For the salsa:

1 avocado, diced

1 cup tomato, chopped

¼ cup white onion,
  chopped

¼ tsp. kosher salt

Squeeze of fresh
  lime juice

1. Preheat the air fryer to 390°F.

2. Place the all-purpose flour, egg, and panko breadcrumbs into 3 separate shallow bowls, then season each with ¼ teaspoon of kosher salt and ¼ teaspoon of black pepper.

3. Dredge the fish strips in the flour, then the egg, and finally the breadcrumbs.

4. Spray the fryer basket with nonstick cooking spray, then drizzle 4 fish strips with 1 tablespoon of canola oil, place in the basket, and cook for 10 minutes.

5. Remove the strips from the basket and place on a wire rack. Repeat this process with the remaining fish strips.

6. While the fish strips cook, make the salsa in a medium bowl by mashing together the avocado, tomato, onion, kosher salt, and lime juice. Set aside.

7. Remove the fish from the fryer and place 2 strips in each corn tortilla, then add ¼ cup of avocado salsa. (You can also use other toppings, like shredded lettuce or hot sauce.) Serve warm.

NUTRITION PER SERVING

Total fat **17g**	Cholesterol **99mg**	Carbohydrates **50g**	Sugars **4g**
Saturated fat **3g**	Sodium **384mg**	Dietary fiber **8g**	Protein **29g**

LIGHTER SIDES

Side dishes can often hide loads of extra calories and fat, but with the air fryer, you can enjoy many savory indulgences, including French fries!

204 CALORIES
PER SERVING

MAKES **4 cups**
SERVING SIZE **2 cups**
PREP TIME **5 minutes**
COOK TIME **12 minutes**
FRYER TEMP **390°F**

With a crispy outside, a soft inside, and the perfect amount of salty crunch, these air fryer French fries are just as delicious as they are healthy.

Classic French Fries

2 russet potatoes, skin on, scrubbed, and patted dry

2 tsp. olive oil

¼ tsp. kosher salt

1. Preheat the air fryer to 390°F.

2. Cut the russet potatoes into fry shapes, then place the fries, olive oil, and kosher salt in a medium bowl and toss.

3. Spray the fryer basket with nonstick cooking spray, then place the fries in the basket and cook for 5 minutes.

4. Pause the fryer, gently shake the basket, and cook for 5–6 more minutes or until crispy and golden brown.

5. Remove the fries from the fryer and allow to cool on a wire rack for 5 minutes before serving.

A large order of restaurant French fries has more than 500 calories and 25 grams of fat!

NUTRITION PER SERVING

Total fat **5g**	Cholesterol **0mg**	Carbohydrates **37g**	Sugars **2g**
Saturated fat **1g**	Sodium **153mg**	Dietary fiber **5g**	Protein **4g**

This ever-popular salad usually doesn't have much to offer in the nutrition department, but this version transforms a classic into a nutrient-filled meal.

Kale Caesar Salad with Croutons

180 CALORIES PER SERVING

MAKES **2 salads**
SERVING SIZE **1 salad**
PREP TIME **10 minutes**
COOK TIME **7 minutes**
FRYER TEMP **360°F**

4 cups kale, chopped and divided

1 tsp. olive oil

1 TB. nonfat plain Greek yogurt

¼ tsp. Dijon mustard

1 TB. grated Parmesan cheese

For the croutons:

1 cup whole grain bread, cubed

2 tsp. olive oil

1. Preheat the air fryer to 360°F.

2. Spray the fryer basket with nonstick cooking spray, then place 1 cup of kale in the basket and cook for 2 minutes or until crispy.

3. While the kale cooks, make the dressing in a large bowl by whisking together the olive oil, plain Greek yogurt, Dijon mustard, and Parmesan cheese. Set aside.

4. Remove the kale from the fryer and place on a plate lined with a paper towel to cool. (Clean the basket before making the croutons.)

5. Make the croutons in a separate large bowl by tossing the bread cubes and olive oil. Place the cubes in the basket and cook for 5 minutes or until golden brown.

6. Remove the croutons from the fryer. Add the cooked and raw kale to the dressing bowl, tossing to combine, then top with the croutons before serving.

NUTRITION PER SERVING

Total fat **8g**	Cholesterol **2mg**	Carbohydrates **23g**	Sugars **5g**
Saturated fat **1g**	Sodium **147mg**	Dietary fiber **6g**	Protein **10g**

169 CALORIES PER SERVING

MAKES **3 cups**
SERVING SIZE **1½ cups**
PREP TIME **5 minutes**
COOK TIME **15 minutes**
FRYER TEMP **360°F**

Sweet potato fries might seem like a healthy option, but many varieties aren't. This version cuts down on the fat and features a burst of flavor from fresh dill.

Sweet Potato Fries with Fresh Dill

1 large sweet potato, peeled

1 TB. canola oil

¼ tsp. kosher salt

2 TB. crumbled feta

2 TB. fresh dill, chopped

1. Preheat the air fryer to 360°F.

2. Cut the sweet potato into ½-inch-thick fry shapes.

3. Place the fries in a medium bowl, add the canola oil and kosher salt, and toss to coat.

4. Spray the fryer basket with nonstick cooking spray, then place the fries in the basket and cook for 15 minutes.

5. Remove the fries from the fryer, place on a plate lined with a paper towel, and sprinkle the feta and dill on top. Allow to cool for 5 minutes before serving.

This saves up to 300 calories per serving compared with typical sweet potato fries.

NUTRITION PER SERVING

Total fat **9g**	Cholesterol **8mg**	Carbohydrates **20g**	Sugars **6g**
Saturated fat **2g**	Sodium **326mg**	Dietary fiber **3g**	Protein **3g**

MAKES **4 ramekins**
SERVING SIZE **1 ramekin**
PREP TIME **10 minutes**
COOK TIME **30 minutes**
FRYER TEMP **330°F**

This savory holiday dish doesn't have to drown in sugary toppings. You can now enjoy this healthy complement to chicken or turkey thanks to the air fryer.

Sweet Potato Soufflé

1 sweet potato, baked and mashed

2 TB. unsalted butter, divided

1 large egg, separated

¼ cup whole milk

½ tsp. kosher salt

1. Preheat the air fryer to 330°F.

2. In a medium bowl, combine the sweet potato, 1 tablespoon of melted butter, egg yolk, milk, and salt. Set aside.

3. In a separate medium bowl, whisk the egg white until stiff peaks form.

4. Using a spatula, gently fold the egg white into the sweet potato mixture.

5. Coat the inside of four 3-inch ramekins with the remaining 1 tablespoon of butter, then fill each ramekin halfway full. Place 2 ramekins in the fryer basket and cook for 15 minutes. Repeat this process with the remaining ramekins.

6. Remove the ramekins from the fryer and allow to cool on a wire rack for 10 minutes before serving.

Skip the cheese-laden soufflé, which can have almost 200 more calories.

NUTRITION PER SERVING

Total fat **7g**	Cholesterol **63mg**	Carbohydrates **10g**	Sugars **4g**
Saturated fat **4g**	Sodium **181mg**	Dietary fiber **1g**	Protein **3g**

Cauliflower has become a trendy superfood. It's low in calories and filled with nutrients, including some that might even help lower your risk of cancer.

Parmesan Cauliflower Cakes

91 CALORIES PER SERVING

MAKES **6**
SERVING SIZE **1**
PREP TIME **10 minutes**
COOK TIME **20 minutes**
FRYER TEMP **390°F**

2 cups cooked cauliflower

1 large egg, beaten

½ cup grated Parmesan cheese

1 TB. fresh chives, chopped

1 cup panko breadcrumbs

1. Preheat the air fryer to 390°F.

2. In a large bowl, combine the cauliflower, egg, Parmesan cheese, chives, and panko breadcrumbs, then use a potato masher to mash the ingredients, retaining a chunky texture.

3. Form the mixture into 6 round cakes, then spray both sides with nonstick cooking spray.

4. Spray the fryer basket with nonstick cooking spray, then place 3 cakes in the basket and cook for 8 minutes. Repeat this process with the remaining cakes.

5. Remove the cakes from the fryer and allow to cool on a wire rack for 5 minutes before serving.

NUTRITION PER SERVING

Total fat **3g**	Cholesterol **38mg**	Carbohydrates **9g**	Sugars **1g**
Saturated fat **2g**	Sodium **160mg**	Dietary fiber **1g**	Protein **6g**

You can enjoy moist and scrumptious cornbread without all the fat. Cheese and jalapeño make this a delightful accompaniment to soup, chili, or BBQ.

Jalapeño & Cheddar Cornbread

120 CALORIES PER SERVING

MAKES **8 squares**
SERVING SIZE **1 square**
PREP TIME **10 minutes**
COOK TIME **20 minutes**
FRYER TEMP **300°F**

⅔ cup cornmeal

⅓ cup all-purpose flour

½ tsp. kosher salt

¾ tsp. baking powder

1 TB. granulated sugar

2 TB. buttery spread, melted

1 large egg, beaten

¾ cup whole milk

⅓ cup shredded sharp cheddar cheese

1 jalapeño pepper, thinly sliced

1. Preheat the air fryer to 300°F.

2. In a large bowl, combine the cornmeal, all-purpose flour, kosher salt, baking powder, and granulated sugar. Use a spatula to fold in the buttery spread, egg, and milk, then fold in the sharp cheddar cheese and jalapeño pepper.

3. Spray the air fryer baking pan with nonstick cooking spray, then pour the mixture into the pan and cook for 20 minutes or until a toothpick comes out clean when inserted in the middle.

4. Remove the cornbread from the fryer and allow to cool in the pan on a wire rack for 10 minutes before cutting. Serve warm.

Traditional cornbread recipes have twice the fat—usually from butter.

NUTRITION PER SERVING

| Total fat **6g** | Cholesterol **32mg** | Carbohydrates **13g** | Sugars **3g** |
| Saturated fat **2g** | Sodium **190mg** | Dietary fiber **1g** | Protein **4g** |

MAKES **48**
SERVING SIZE **12**
PREP TIME **5 minutes**
COOK TIME **20 minutes**
FRYER TEMP **360°F**

Turn a simple zucchini into something amazing!
These tender and sweet fries have just the right
amount of crunch to satisfy even picky eaters.

Zucchini Fries

1 medium zucchini,
cut into 48 sticks

1 TB. buttery spread,
melted

¼ cup seasoned
breadcrumbs

1. Preheat the air fryer to 360°F.

2. Place the buttery spread and the seasoned
   breadcrumbs into 2 separate shallow dishes.

3. Dip the zucchini sticks in the buttery spread, then into
   the breadcrumbs. Place the coated sticks on a plate.

4. Spray the air fryer basket with nonstick cooking spray,
   then place half the sticks in the fryer and cook for
   10 minutes or until crispy. Repeat this process with
   the remaining sticks.

5. Remove the fries from the fryer and allow to cool on
   a wire rack for 5 minutes before serving.

NUTRITION PER SERVING

Total fat **3g**	Cholesterol **0mg**	Carbohydrates **7g**	Sugars **3g**
Saturated fat **1g**	Sodium **209mg**	Dietary fiber **1g**	Protein **2g**

Enjoy these irresistibly crunchy eggplant slices with a squeeze of fresh lemon or pair them with marinara sauce for dipping.

Panko-Crusted Eggplant

113 CALORIES PER SERVING

MAKES **8–10 pieces**
SERVING SIZE **2 pieces**
PREP TIME **15 minutes**
COOK TIME **35 minutes**
FRYER TEMP **360°F**

½ cup all-purpose flour

1 large egg, beaten

2 cups panko breadcrumbs

1 tsp. kosher salt (plus extra for serving)

1 tsp. freshly ground black pepper

2 TB. canola oil

1 medium eggplant, sliced

1. Preheat the air fryer to 360°F.

2. Place the all-purpose flour, egg, and panko breadcrumbs into 3 separate shallow bowls, then season each with equal parts kosher salt and black pepper. Stir the canola oil into the breadcrumbs.

3. Dredge each eggplant slice in the flour, then the egg, and finally the breadcrumbs. Shake off any excess, then place each coated slice on a plate

4. Spray the fryer basket with nonstick cooking spray, then place 2–3 eggplant slices in the basket and cook for 6 minutes or until crispy and golden brown. Repeat this process with the remaining slices.

5. Remove the eggplant from the fryer and place on a wire rack, then season with a pinch of kosher salt. Serve warm.

NUTRITION PER SERVING

Total fat **5g**	Cholesterol **47mg**	Carbohydrates **15g**	Sugars **5g**
Saturated fat **1g**	Sodium **172mg**	Dietary fiber **4g**	Protein **4g**

Spiralized vegetables are a great way to enjoy your favorite pasta dishes without all the calories. If you don't have a spiralizer, use a julienne peeler instead.

Zoodles with Garlic Oil

70 CALORIES PER SERVING

MAKES **4 cups**
SERVING SIZE **1 cup**
PREP TIME **5 minutes**
COOK TIME **10 minutes**
FRYER TEMP **360°F**

2 large yellow summer squash, peeled and spiralized

2 large zucchini, peeled and spiralized

1 TB. olive oil, divided

½ tsp. kosher salt

1 garlic clove, whole

2 TB. fresh basil, chopped

1. Preheat the air fryer to 360°F.

2. Place the squash and zucchini in a medium bowl, then season with 1 teaspoon of olive oil and the kosher salt.

3. Spray the fryer basket with nonstick cooking spray, then place the squash, zucchini, and garlic clove in the basket and cook for 10 minutes.

4. Remove the squash and zucchini from the fryer and return to the medium bowl. Set aside.

5. Remove the garlic clove from the fryer and mince well.

6. Make the garlic oil in a small bowl by combining the minced garlic with the remaining 2 teaspoons of olive oil.

7. Add the garlic oil to the squash and zucchini bowl, tossing to combine, and sprinkle the basil on top. Serve warm.

NUTRITION PER SERVING

Total fat **7g**	Cholesterol **0mg**	Carbohydrates **8g**	Sugars **5g**
Saturated fat **4g**	Sodium **145mg**	Dietary fiber **3g**	Protein **3g**

134 CALORIES PER SERVING

MAKES **1 slice**
SERVING SIZE **1 slice**
PREP TIME **2 minutes**
COOK TIME **10 minutes**
FRYER TEMP **330°F**

Move over garlic bread—this healthier version offers nutrients not found in white bread. Serve this with a lean protein and veggies for a complete meal.

Whole Wheat Cheesy Bread

1 slice whole wheat bread

1 garlic clove, peeled

2 TB. shredded part-skim mozzarella cheese

1. Preheat the air fryer to 330°F.

2. Spray the fryer basket with nonstick cooking spray, then place the whole wheat bread in the basket and cook for 2 minutes.

3. Pause the fryer, remove the bread from the basket, and rub it gently with the garlic clove.

4. Return the bread to the basket, top with the mozzarella cheese, and cook for 5 more minutes or until the cheese melts.

5. Remove the bread from the fryer and allow to cool on a wire rack for 5 minutes before serving.

This has half the fat of other cheesy breads and 75 fewer calories than garlic bread.

NUTRITION PER SERVING

Total fat **5g**	Cholesterol **8mg**	Carbohydrates **18g**	Sugars **1g**
Saturated fat **2g**	Sodium **206mg**	Dietary fiber **2g**	Protein **6g**

This unusual pairing looks complex and elegant but couldn't be easier to make. This makes a great addition to grilled chicken or smoked salmon.

90 CALORIES PER SERVING

MAKES **3 cups**
SERVING SIZE **¾ cup**
PREP TIME **10 minutes**
COOK TIME **20 minutes**
FRYER TEMP **300°F/360°F**

Butternut Squash with Hazelnuts

2 TB. whole hazelnuts

3 cups butternut squash, peeled, seeded, and cubed

2 tsp. olive oil

¼ tsp. kosher salt

¼ tsp. freshly ground black pepper

1. Preheat the air fryer to 300°F.

2. Spray the fryer basket with nonstick cooking spray, then place the hazelnuts in the basket and cook for 3 minutes.

3. Remove the hazelnuts from the fryer, roughly chop, and place in small bowl. Set aside. (Clean the basket before cooking the squash.)

4. Preheat the air fryer to 360°F.

5. Toss the butternut squash with the olive oil, kosher salt, and black pepper.

6. Spray the basket with nonstick cooking spray, then place the squash in the basket and cook for 20 minutes or until fork tender.

7. Remove the squash from the fryer, place in a serving bowl, and sprinkle the hazelnuts on top. Serve warm.

NUTRITION PER SERVING

Total fat **5g**	Cholesterol **0mg**	Carbohydrates **13g**	Sugars **2g**
Saturated fat **1g**	Sodium **74mg**	Dietary fiber **2g**	Protein **2g**

Beets are one of the healthiest foods on the planet and high in antioxidants. If you're unsure whether you're a fan of beets, this will help convince you.

Beet Salad with Lemon & Chive Vinaigrette

136 CALORIES PER SERVING.

MAKES **10 cups**
SERVING SIZE **2½ cups**
PREP TIME **10 minutes**
COOK TIME **15 minutes**
FRYER TEMP **360°F**

6 medium red
and golden beets,
peeled and sliced

1 tsp. olive oil

¼ tsp. kosher salt

½ cup crumbled
feta cheese

8 cups mixed greens

For the vinaigrette:

2 tsp. olive oil

2 TB. fresh chives,
chopped

Juice of 1 lemon

1. Preheat the air fryer to 360°F.

2. In a large bowl, toss the beets, olive oil, and kosher salt.

3. Spray the fryer basket with nonstick cooking spray, then place the beets in the basket and cook for 12–15 minutes or until tender.

4. While the beets cook, make the vinaigrette in a large bowl by whisking together the olive oil, lemon juice, and chives.

5. Remove the beets from the fryer, toss in the vinaigrette, and allow to cool for 5 minutes. Add the feta and serve on top of the mixed greens.

NUTRITION PER SERVING

Total fat **8g**	Cholesterol **17mg**	Carbohydrates **13g**	Sugars **8g**
Saturated fat **3g**	Sodium **342mg**	Dietary fiber **4g**	Protein **5g**

MAKES **4 cups**
SERVING SIZE **1 cup**
PREP TIME **10 minutes**
COOK TIME **10 minutes**
FRYER TEMP **360°F**

Parsnips are an underappreciated root veggie, and these fries boast enough fiber to help curb hunger while satisfying a salty snack craving.

Parsnip Fries with Creamy Roasted Garlic Dip

3 medium parsnips, peeled

1 tsp. olive oil

¼ tsp. kosher salt

1 garlic clove, unpeeled

For the dipping sauce:

¼ cup nonfat plain Greek yogurt

1 TB. sour cream

¼ tsp. kosher salt

⅛ tsp. garlic powder

Freshly ground black pepper

1. Preheat the air fryer to 360°F.

2. Cut the parsnips into fry shapes, then place in a medium bowl, toss with the olive oil, and season with the kosher salt.

3. Spray the fryer basket with nonstick cooking spray, then place the parsnips and garlic clove in the basket and cook for 5 minutes.

4. Pause the fryer to remove the garlic clove from the basket, then peel and mash it. Shake the basket and cook the fries for 3–5 more minutes.

5. While the fries cook, make the dipping sauce in a medium bowl by combining the mashed garlic, plain Greek yogurt, sour cream, kosher salt, and garlic powder. Set aside.

6. Remove the fries from the fryer, place on a wire rack, and season with black pepper. Serve warm with the dipping sauce on the side.

NUTRITION PER SERVING

Total fat **2g**	Cholesterol **3mg**	Carbohydrates **21g**	Sugars **6g**
Saturated fat **1g**	Sodium **159mg**	Dietary fiber **4g**	Protein **3g**

This healthier take on a traditional corn casserole—often a holiday staple—is bursting with flavor that features a cayenne pepper kick.

Corn Casserole

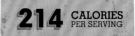

214 CALORIES PER SERVING

MAKES **4 cups**
SERVING SIZE **1 cup**
PREP TIME **10 minutes**
COOK TIME **20 minutes**
FRYER TEMP **330°F**

½ cup all-purpose flour

½ cup yellow cornmeal

1 TB. granulated sugar

½ tsp. baking powder

¼ tsp. kosher salt

Pinch of cayenne pepper

2 TB. melted unsalted butter

½ cup low-fat milk

1 large egg, beaten

1 cup corn kernels

¼ cup bell pepper, finely chopped

1. Preheat the air fryer to 330°F.

2. In a large bowl, combine the all-purpose flour, yellow cornmeal, granulated sugar, baking powder, kosher salt, and cayenne pepper. Stir in the butter, low-fat milk, and egg, then fold in the corn kernels and bell pepper.

3. Spray the air fryer baking pan with nonstick cooking spray, then pour the mixture into the pan and cook for 20 minutes.

4. Remove the casserole from the fryer and allow to cool in the pan on a wire rack for 10 minutes before serving.

Using corn kernels rather than creamed corn saves almost 150 calories.

NUTRITION PER SERVING

Total fat **8g**	Cholesterol **63mg**	Carbohydrates **31g**	Sugars **3g**
Saturated fat **4g**	Sodium **166mg**	Dietary fiber **3g**	Protein **6g**

287 CALORIES PER SERVING

MAKES **24 balls**
SERVING SIZE **4 balls**
PREP TIME **60 minutes**
COOK TIME **40 minutes**
FRYER TEMP **390°F**

This classic Sicilian recipe is often as high in calories as it is in taste, but you can make it in the air fryer—and enjoy it without all the guilt!

Arancini with Marinara

1½ cups cooked Arborio rice

¼ cup grated Parmesan cheese

¼ cup shredded part-skim mozzarella cheese

1 large egg, beaten

½ tsp. kosher salt

¼ tsp. freshly ground black pepper

½ cup seasoned breadcrumbs

1 TB. olive oil

½ cup panko breadcrumbs

For the sauce:

2 TB. olive oil

1 garlic clove, minced

1 (28 oz.) can crushed tomatoes

½ tsp. kosher salt

1. In a large bowl, combine the cooked Arborio rice, Parmesan and mozzarella cheeses, egg, kosher salt, black pepper, and seasoned breadcrumbs. Place the rice mixture in the refrigerator for 30 minutes.

2. To make the sauce, place the olive oil in a saucepan and heat on low, then add the minced garlic and sauté for 1 minute. Stir in the tomatoes and kosher salt, then simmer for 20 minutes. Set aside.

3. Preheat the air fryer to 390°F.

4. In a small bowl, combine the olive oil and panko breadcrumbs. Use clean hands to roll 1 tablespoon of the rice mixture into a small ball, then roll in the panko mixture. Repeat this process with the remaining rice mixture. (Keep your hands wet to help form the balls.)

5. Spray the fryer basket with nonstick cooking spray, then place 5–6 rice balls in the basket and cook for 8 minutes or until golden brown. Repeat this process with the remaining balls.

6. Remove the arancini from the fryer and place on a wire rack. Serve warm with the sauce on the side for dipping.

NUTRITION PER SERVING

Total fat **12g**	Cholesterol **39mg**	Carbohydrates **34g**	Sugars **6g**
Saturated fat **3g**	Sodium **535mg**	Dietary fiber **3g**	Protein **9g**

149 CALORIES PER SERVING

MAKES **16**
SERVING SIZE **8**
PREP TIME **15 minutes**
COOK TIME **10–15 minutes**
FRYER TEMP **390°F**

Forget about trying to satisfy your onion ring craving at a fast-food restaurant on from a deep fryer. You can make a healthier version in the air fryer.

Golden Onion Rings

1 white or Vidalia onion, peeled and sliced ½-inch thick

½ cup all-purpose flour

1 cup low-fat buttermilk

1 cup panko breadcrumbs

1 TB. canola oil

1. Preheat the air fryer to 390°F.

2. Separate the onion slices into rings, then place the all-purpose flour and the slices in a sealable plastic bag, shaking to coat. Set aside.

3. Place the low-fat buttermilk and panko breadcrumbs into 2 separate shallow bowls, then stir the canola oil into the breadcrumbs.

4. Using clean hands, remove an onion ring from the flour, dip it into the buttermilk, and coat with the panko mixture. Place each coated onion ring on a plate, then repeat this process with the remaining onion rings.

5. Spray the fryer basket with nonstick cooking spray, then place 5–6 onion rings in the basket and cook for 5 minutes. Repeat this process with the remaining onion rings.

6. Remove the onion rings from the fryer, place on a wire rack, and serve warm.

A similar serving of deep-fried onion rings is almost 500 calories!

NUTRITION PER SERVING

Total fat **6g**	Cholesterol **3mg**	Carbohydrates **20g**	Sugars **4g**
Saturated fat **1g**	Sodium **178mg**	Dietary fiber **1g**	Protein **4g**

Green beans cooked in the air fryer are sweet and tender—and have just a little crunch. This addictive treat might change your mind about eating veggies.

Crunchy Green Beans

55 CALORIES PER SERVING

MAKES **3 cups**
SERVING SIZE **1½ cups**
PREP TIME **2 minutes**
COOK TIME **5 minutes**
FRYER TEMP **390°F**

8 oz. fresh green beans
1 tsp. canola oil
¼ tsp. kosher salt

1. Preheat the air fryer to 390°F.

2. Spray the fryer basket with nonstick cooking spray. In a medium bowl, toss the green beans and canola oil, place the beans in the basket, and cook for 5 minutes.

3. Remove the green beans from the fryer, place on a serving dish, and sprinkle with the kosher salt. Serve warm.

NUTRITION PER SERVING

Total fat **3g**	Cholesterol **0mg**	Carbohydrates **8g**	Sugars **4g**
Saturated fat **0g**	Sodium **147mg**	Dietary fiber **3g**	Protein **2g**

Most restaurants feature greasy and calorie-laden Brussels sprouts as appetizers. But these are light, crunchy—and absolutely delicious!

Soy-Glazed Brussels Sprouts

69 CALORIES PER SERVING

MAKES **2 cups**
SERVING SIZE **½ cup**
PREP TIME **5 minutes**
COOK TIME **12 minutes**
FRYER TEMP **330°F**

12 oz. Brussels sprouts, gently trimmed and quartered

2 tsp. sesame oil

1 TB. maple syrup

1 TB. reduced-sodium soy sauce

1. Preheat the fryer to 330°F.

2. Place the Brussels sprouts in a large bowl and set aside.

3. In a small bowl, whisk together the sesame oil, maple syrup, and soy sauce, then add the soy glaze to the Brussels sprouts, tossing to coat.

4. Spray the fryer basket with nonstick cooking spray, then place the Brussels sprouts in the basket and cook for 12 minutes.

5. Remove the Brussels sprouts from the fryer, place on a serving plate, and allow to cool for 5 minutes before serving.

NUTRITION PER SERVING

| Total fat **3g** | Cholesterol **0mg** | Carbohydrates **10g** | Sugars **3g** |
| Saturated fat **0g** | Sodium **84mg** | Dietary fiber **3g** | Protein **3g** |

MAKES **2 cups**
SERVING SIZE **½ cup**
PREP TIME **10 minutes**
COOK TIME **20 minutes**
FRYER TEMP **330°F**

Glazed carrots are wonderful when served on their own or as a sweet salad topper. Air-frying them will keep them crispy and help retain all their nutrients.

Glazed Carrots

3 cups carrots, peeled and sliced (1-inch thick)

1 TB. honey

3 TB. water

1. Preheat the air fryer to 330°F.

2. Spray the air fryer baking pan with nonstick cooking spray, then place the carrots in the pan and cook for 10 minutes.

3. Pause the fryer, stir the honey and water into the pan, and cook for 5 more minutes or until the water is absorbed and the carrots are tender.

4. Remove the carrots from the fryer, place in a serving dish, and allow to cool for 5 minutes before serving.

NUTRITION PER SERVING

Total fat **0g**	Cholesterol **0mg**	Carbohydrates **14g**	Sugars **9g**
Saturated fat **0g**	Sodium **66mg**	Dietary fiber **3g**	Protein **1g**

Air-fried tomatoes feature a juicy, sweet piquancy. These jewel-like tomatoes are ready in minutes and make a fantastically delicious, low-calorie side dish.

Cherry Tomatoes & Garlic with Basil

49 CALORIES PER SERVING

MAKES **1½ cups**
SERVING SIZE **¾ cup**
PREP TIME **5 minutes**
COOK TIME **10 minutes**
FRYER TEMP **360°F**

2 cups cherry tomatoes

1 tsp. olive oil

1 garlic clove, peeled and thinly sliced

⅛ tsp. kosher salt

1 TB. fresh basil, chopped (for serving)

1. Preheat the air fryer to 360°F.

2. Spray the air fryer baking pan with nonstick cooking spray, then place the cherry tomatoes, olive oil, sliced garlic, and kosher salt in the pan and gently stir.

3. Cook for 4–6 minutes or until the tomatoes begin to burst.

4. Remove the tomatoes and any garlic from the fryer, place on a serving dish, and allow to cool for 5 minutes. Sprinkle the basil on top and serve warm.

NUTRITION PER SERVING

Total fat **3g**	Cholesterol **0mg**	Carbohydrates **6g**	Sugars **4g**
Saturated fat **0g**	Sodium **78mg**	Dietary fiber **2g**	Protein **1g**

WHOLESOME SNACKS

Snacking can be difficult when you're trying to eat healthier, but the air fryer lets you enjoy snacks that taste better *and* are healthier than any pub grub.

MAKES **4**
SERVING SIZE **1**
PREP TIME **10 minutes**
COOK TIME **10 minutes**
FRYER TEMP **360°F**

These mini pizzas are loaded with flavor and will satisfy even the strongest of snack cravings—without a calorie overload.

Personal Sausage Pizzas

2 oz. pizza dough (see page 52)

2 TB. marinara sauce (see page 98)

2 oz. provolone cheese, torn into pieces

2 links breakfast sausage, thinly sliced

1 bunch fresh parsley, chopped (for serving)

1. Preheat the air fryer to 360°F.

2. Separate the dough into 4 balls and roll out each ball on a lightly floured surface.

3. Top each pizza with equal amounts of marinara sauce, provolone cheese, and sausage.

4. Spray the fryer basket with nonstick cooking spray, then place 2 pizzas in the basket and cook for 5 minutes. Repeat this process with the remaining pizzas.

5. Remove the pizzas from the fryer, sprinkle the parsley on top, and allow to cool on a wire rack for 5 minutes before serving.

This pizza recipe will save you almost 200 calories per slice.

NUTRITION PER SERVING

Total fat **6g**	Cholesterol **16mg**	Carbohydrates **7g**	Sugars **1g**
Saturated fat **3g**	Sodium **290mg**	Dietary fiber **0g**	Protein **6g**

Air-frying some fresh corn tortillas creates a lighter version of this snack that has fewer calories and less fat but still retains that satisfying salty crunch.

71 CALORIES
PER SERVING

MAKES **24**
SERVING SIZE **6**
PREP TIME **5 minutes**
COOK TIME **10 minutes**
FRYER TEMP **360°F**

Corn Tortilla Chips

4 six-inch corn tortillas
1 TB. canola oil
¼ tsp. kosher salt

1. Preheat the air fryer to 360°F.

2. Stack the corn tortillas, cut in half, then slice into thirds.

3. Spray the fryer basket with nonstick cooking spray, then brush the tortillas with canola oil and place in the basket. Cook for 5 minutes.

4. Pause the fryer to shake the basket, then cook for 3–5 more minutes or until golden brown and crispy.

5. Remove the chips from the fryer and place on a plate lined with a paper towel. Sprinkle the kosher salt on top before serving warm.

Twice the number of deep-fried chips also have twice the calories.

NUTRITION PER SERVING

| Total fat **4g** | Cholesterol **0mg** | Carbohydrates **8g** | Sugars **0g** |
| Saturated fat **0g** | Sodium **79mg** | Dietary fiber **1g** | Protein **1g** |

MAKES **8**

SERVING SIZE **1**

PREP TIME **20 minutes**

COOK TIME **65 minutes**

FRYER TEMP **360°F**

This recipe makes this popular pub food healthier by piling on the cauliflower and using a sensible amount of cheese. It will please a crowd every time!

Cauliflower & Cheddar Potato Skins

4 medium russet
 potatoes, washed

2 TB. olive oil

½ tsp. kosher salt

½ tsp. freshly ground
 black pepper

1 cup cauliflower florets,
 finely chopped

½ cup shredded
 sharp cheddar cheese

2 TB. fresh chives,
 chopped (for serving)

1. Preheat the air fryer to 360°F.

2. Spray the fryer basket with nonstick cooking spray, then place 2 potatoes in the basket and cook for 20 minutes or until tender. Repeat this process with the remaining potatoes.

3. Remove the potatoes from the fryer, then once the potatoes are cool enough to handle, cut in half lengthwise and scoop out some of the flesh.

4. Brush the insides of the potato skins with olive oil, then season with the kosher salt and black pepper.

5. Top each potato skin with 2 tablespoons of cauliflower and 1 tablespoon of shredded cheddar cheese.

6. Place 4 potato skins in the basket and cook for 12 minutes. Repeat this process with the remaining potato skins.

7. Remove the potato skins from the fryer, place on a serving plate, and sprinkle the chives on top. Allow to cool for 5 minutes before serving.

A restaurant order of loaded potato skins has more than 1,000 calories!

NUTRITION PER SERVING

Total fat **5g**	Cholesterol **5mg**	Carbohydrates **12g**	Sugars **1g**
Saturated fat **2g**	Sodium **111mg**	Dietary fiber **3g**	Protein **3g**

Fried pickles are a Southern delicacy! But instead of a heavy, high-fat batter, these pickle chips have a thin layer of breading—plus a kick of Cajun spice.

Crispy Cajun Pickle Chips

¼ cup all-purpose flour

½ cup panko breadcrumbs

1 large egg, beaten

2 tsp. Cajun seasoning

2 large dill pickles, sliced into 8 rounds each

1. Preheat the air fryer to 390°F.

2. Place the all-purpose flour, panko breadcrumbs, and egg into 3 separate shallow bowls, then stir the Cajun seasoning into the flour.

3. Dredge each pickle chip in the flour mixture, then the egg, and finally the breadcrumbs. Shake off any excess, then place each coated pickle chip on a plate.

4. Spray the air fryer basket with nonstick cooking spray, then place 8 pickle chips in the basket and cook for 5 minutes or until crispy and golden brown. Repeat this process with the remaining pickle chips.

5. Remove the chips from the fryer and allow to slightly cool on a wire rack before serving.

A similar serving size of deep-fried pickles has 250 calories and 12 grams of fat!

NUTRITION PER SERVING

Total fat **1g**	Cholesterol **47mg**	Carbohydrates **11g**	Sugars **1g**
Saturated fat **0g**	Sodium **598mg**	Dietary fiber **1g**	Protein **3g**

Serve these spicy bites as a snack at a gathering or as part of a meal. You can also enjoy them on a salad, in a wrap, or as a pizza topping.

Buffalo Chicken Bites

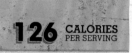

126 CALORIES PER SERVING

MAKES **30**
SERVING SIZE **15**
PREP TIME **10 minutes**
COOK TIME **10–12 minutes**
FRYER TEMP **390°F**

8 oz. boneless and skinless chicken thighs, cut into 30 pieces

¼ tsp. kosher salt

2 TB. hot sauce

1. Preheat the air fryer to 390°F.

2. Spray the fryer basket with nonstick cooking spray and season the chicken bites with the kosher salt, then place in the basket and cook for 10–12 minutes or until crispy.

3. While the chicken bites cook, pour the hot sauce into a large bowl.

4. Remove the bites from the fryer and add to the sauce bowl, tossing to coat. Serve warm.

NUTRITION PER SERVING

| Total fat **9g** | Cholesterol **56mg** | Carbohydrates **56g** | Sugars **0g** |
| Saturated fat **2g** | Sodium **161mg** | Dietary fiber **0g** | Protein **9g** |

Make a batch of these chicken wings for your next backyard BBQ or game day celebration. Sriracha and honey give them a spicy–sweet kick!

Sriracha Honey Chicken Wings

167 CALORIES PER SERVING

MAKES **16**
SERVING SIZE **4**
PREP TIME **5 minutes**
COOK TIME **30 minutes**
FRYER TEMP **360°F**

1 TB. Sriracha hot sauce

1 TB. honey

1 garlic clove, minced

½ tsp. kosher salt

16 chicken wings
and drumettes

1. Preheat the air fryer to 360°F.

2. In a large bowl, whisk together the Sriracha hot sauce, honey, minced garlic, and kosher salt, then add the chicken and toss to coat.

3. Spray the fryer basket with nonstick cooking spray, then place 8 wings in the basket and cook for 15 minutes, turning halfway through. Repeat this process with the remaining wings.

4. Remove the wings from the fryer and allow to cool on a wire rack for 10 minutes before serving.

This recipe cuts the calories of fried chicken wings by more than 400 per serving.

NUTRITION PER SERVING

| Total fat **4g** | Cholesterol **66mg** | Carbohydrates **5g** | Sugars **5g** |
| Saturated fat **1g** | Sodium **309mg** | Dietary fiber **0g** | Protein **26g** |

Spicy jalapeño peppers with a gooey cheese filling are fantastic for anyone who loves things hot! The air fryer allows you to make them quickly—and deliciously!

Jalapeño Poppers

8 jalapeño peppers

½ cup whipped cream cheese

¼ cup shredded cheddar cheese

1. Preheat the air fryer to 360°F.

2. Use a paring knife to carefully cut off the jalapeño tops, then scoop out the ribs and seeds. Set aside.

3. In a medium bowl, combine the whipped cream cheese and shredded cheddar cheese. Place the mixture in a sealable plastic bag, and using a pair of scissors, cut off one corner from the bag. Gently squeeze some cream cheese mixture into each pepper until almost full.

4. Place a piece of parchment paper on the bottom of the fryer basket and place the poppers on top, distributing evenly. (The air from the fryer will move the paper around some but won't disrupt the cooking.) Cook for 10 minutes.

5. Allow the poppers to cool in the fryer for 5–10 minutes before serving.

Using whipped cream cheese means 20% fewer calories than regular cream cheese.

NUTRITION PER SERVING

Total fat **8g**	Cholesterol **26mg**	Carbohydrates **3g**	Sugars **2g**
Saturated fat **5g**	Sodium **141mg**	Dietary fiber **1g**	Protein **3g**

Take chicken fingers to a whole new level with the air fryer! Coat crispy tenders in a sweet and tangy sauce for a truly craveable take on chicken wings.

364 CALORIES PER SERVING

MAKES **12**
SERVING SIZE **4**
PREP TIME **5 minutes**
COOK TIME **6–8 minutes**
FRYER TEMP **300°F**

Boneless BBQ Wings

¼ cup BBQ sauce

1 tsp. balsamic vinegar

1 batch Chicken Fingers (see page 62)

1. Preheat the air fryer to 300°F.

2. In a small bowl, whisk together the BBQ sauce and vinegar, then use a brush to coat the Chicken Fingers with an even layer of sauce.

3. Spray the fryer basket with nonstick cooking spray, then place 3–4 boneless wings in the basket and cook for 2 minutes. Repeat this process with the remaining boneless wings.

4. Remove the wings from the fryer and place on a serving plate. Serve warm.

A restaurant serving of 6 wings will set you back more than 600 calories!

NUTRITION PER SERVING

Total fat **11g**	Cholesterol **176mg**	Carbohydrates **19g**	Sugars **2g**
Saturated fat **2g**	Sodium **325mg**	Dietary fiber **1g**	Protein **43g**

These savory tots are the perfect quick snack to make during summer months, when zucchinis are in season. Kids and adults alike will love this healthy finger food.

Zucchini Tots

1 large zucchini, grated

1 medium baked potato, skin removed and mashed

¼ cup shredded cheddar cheese

1 large egg, beaten

½ tsp. kosher salt

1. Preheat the air fryer to 390°F.

2. Wrap the grated zucchini in a paper towel and squeeze out any excess liquid, then combine the zucchini, baked potato, shredded cheddar cheese, egg, and kosher salt in a large bowl.

3. Spray the air fryer baking pan with nonstick cooking spray, then place individual tablespoons of the zucchini mixture in the pan and cook for 10 minutes. Repeat this process with the remaining mixture.

4. Remove the tots from the fryer and allow to cool on a wire rack for 5 minutes before serving.

This recipe cuts out almost 200 calories from a typical serving of deep-fried potatoes.

NUTRITION PER SERVING

Total fat **4g**	Cholesterol **54mg**	Carbohydrates **10g**	Sugars **2g**
Saturated fat **2g**	Sodium **215mg**	Dietary fiber **2g**	Protein **5g**

Small bites of hot dog surrounded by a thick corn batter will make kids—and adults—swoon for this healthier take on a carnival classic.

Corn Dog Bites

½ cup all-purpose flour

½ cup yellow cornmeal

½ tsp. baking powder

¼ tsp. kosher salt

2 TB. buttery spread, melted

6 TB. low-fat milk

2 tsp. honey

1 hot dog, cut into 8 pieces

1. Preheat the air fryer to 390°F.

2. In a large bowl, combine the all-purpose flour, yellow cornmeal, baking powder, and kosher salt, then add the buttery spread, milk, and honey, stirring until it starts to form a ball of soft dough.

3. Divide the dough until you have 8 equal balls, then press each hot dog piece into a ball, making sure to completely encase the piece in the cornmeal dough. Repeat this process with the remaining dough and hot dog pieces.

4. Spray the fryer basket with nonstick cooking spray, then place 4–5 bites in the basket and cook for 6 minutes or until golden brown. Repeat this process with the remaining bites.

5. Remove the bites from the fryer and place on a wire rack. Serve warm.

Typical corn dogs have 15–20 grams of fat per serving.

NUTRITION PER SERVING

Total fat **5g**	Cholesterol **5mg**	Carbohydrates **26g**	Sugars **4g**
Saturated fat **2g**	Sodium **276mg**	Dietary fiber **2g**	Protein **5g**

Want to eat more leafy greens but aren't sure how to prepare them? Flavor kale with smoked paprika for a delicious snack that's ready in minutes.

Smoky Kale Chips

62 CALORIES
PER SERVING

MAKES **4 cups**
SERVING SIZE **1 cup**
PREP TIME **5 minutes**
COOK TIME **8-12 minutes**
FRYER TEMP **390°F**

5 cups kale, large stems removed and chopped

2 tsp. canola oil

¼ tsp. smoked paprika

¼ tsp. kosher salt

1. Preheat the air fryer to 390°F.
2. In a large bowl, toss the kale, canola oil, smoked paprika, and kosher salt.
3. Spray the fryer basket with nonstick cooking spray, then place half the kale in the basket and cook for 2–3 minutes.
4. Pause the fryer, shake the basket, and cook for 2–3 more minutes or until crispy. Repeat this process with the remaining kale.
5. Remove the kale from the fryer and allow to cool on a wire rack for 3–5 minutes before serving.

A serving of regular potato chips has more than 150 calories and 10 grams of fat!

NUTRITION PER SERVING

Total fat **3g**	Cholesterol **0mg**	Carbohydrates **9g**	Sugars **2g**
Saturated fat **0g**	Sodium **184mg**	Dietary fiber **2g**	Protein **3g**

You can make this delectable snack in minutes. Cashews contain healthy fat, but they're totally addictive, so don't feel guilty eating them.

203 CALORIES PER SERVING

MAKES **2 cups**
SERVING SIZE **¼ cup**
PREP TIME **5 minutes**
COOK TIME **5 minutes**
FRYER TEMP **300°F**

Rosemary Cashews

2 sprigs of fresh rosemary (1 chopped and 1 whole)

1 tsp. olive oil

1 tsp. kosher salt

½ tsp. honey

2 cups whole cashews, roasted and unsalted

1. Preheat the air fryer to 300°F.

2. In a medium bowl, whisk together the chopped rosemary, olive oil, kosher salt, and honey. Set aside.

3. Spray the fryer basket with nonstick cooking spray, then place the cashews and the whole rosemary sprig in the basket and cook for 3 minutes.

4. Remove the cashews and rosemary from the fryer, then discard the rosemary and add the cashews to the olive oil mixture, tossing to coat. Allow to cool for 15 minutes before serving.

NUTRITION PER SERVING

Total fat **16g**	Cholesterol **0mg**	Carbohydrates **11g**	Sugars **2g**
Saturated fat **3g**	Sodium **146mg**	Dietary fiber **1g**	Protein **5g**

138 CALORIES PER SERVING

MAKES **3 cups**
SERVING SIZE **¾ cup**
PREP TIME **5 minutes**
COOK TIME **10 minutes**
FRYER TEMP **360°F**

Your guests won't resist diving into this all-star appetizer. Lightened with a few healthy swaps, this dip can help keep calories in check.

Spinach Artichoke Dip

1 (14 oz.) can artichoke hearts packed in water, drained and chopped

1 (10 oz.) package frozen spinach, thawed and drained

1 tsp. minced garlic

2 TB. mayonnaise

¼ cup nonfat plain Greek yogurt

¼ cup shredded part-skim mozzarella cheese

¼ cup grated Parmesan cheese

¼ tsp. freshly ground black pepper

1. Preheat the air fryer to 360°F.

2. Wrap the artichoke hearts and spinach in a paper towel and squeeze out any excess liquid, then transfer the vegetables to a large bowl.

3. Add the minced garlic, mayonnaise, plain Greek yogurt, and mozzarella and Parmesan cheeses to the large bowl, stirring well to combine.

4. Spray the air fryer baking pan with nonstick cooking spray, then transfer the dip mixture to the pan and cook for 10 minutes.

5. Remove the dip from the fryer and allow to cool in the pan on a wire rack for 10 minutes before serving.

This dip at a restaurant has more than 1,200 calories and nearly a day's worth of sodium!

NUTRITION PER SERVING

Total fat **8g**	Cholesterol **12mg**	Carbohydrates **6g**	Sugars **1g**
Saturated fat **2g**	Sodium **270mg**	Dietary fiber **5g**	Protein **8g**

These chips taste better than anything from a bag—and they're also a whole lot healthier! You can make these extra thin and crispy by using a mandoline slicer.

Root Veggie Chips with Herb Salt

74 CALORIES PER SERVING

MAKES **4 cups**
SERVING SIZE **2 cups**
PREP TIME **10 minutes**
COOK TIME **8 minutes**
FRYER TEMP **360°F**

1 parsnip, washed

1 small beet, washed

1 small turnip, washed

½ small sweet potato, washed

1 tsp. olive oil

For the herb salt:

¼ tsp. kosher salt

2 tsp. fresh parsley, finely chopped

1. Preheat the air fryer to 360°F.

2. Peel and thinly slice the parsnip, beet, turnip, and sweet potato, then place the vegetables in a large bowl, add the olive oil, and toss.

3. Spray the fryer basket with nonstick cooking spray, then place the vegetables in the basket and cook for 8 minutes, pausing the fryer halfway through to gently shake the basket.

4. While the chips cook, make the herb salt in a small bowl by combining the kosher salt and parsley.

5. Remove the chips from the fryer and place on a serving plate, then sprinkle the herb salt on top and allow to cool for 2–3 minutes before serving. (They'll become a little crisper as they cool.)

NUTRITION PER SERVING

Total fat **2g**	Cholesterol **0mg**	Carbohydrates **15g**	Sugars **5g**
Saturated fat **0g**	Sodium **225mg**	Dietary fiber **4g**	Protein **1g**

83 CALORIES
PER SERVING

MAKES **12**
SERVING SIZE **2**
PREP TIME **10 minutes**
COOK TIME **10–14 minutes**
FRYER TEMP **360°F**

How can you not love a snack with two ingredients, especially when one of them is bacon? Serve these with almonds and grapes for a balanced snack plate.

Bacon-Wrapped Dates

6 slices high-quality bacon, cut in half

12 dates, pitted

1. Preheat the air fryer to 360°F.

2. Wrap each date with half a bacon slice and secure with a toothpick.

3. Spray the fryer basket with nonstick cooking spray, then place 6 bacon-wrapped dates in the basket and cook for 5–7 minutes or until the bacon is crispy. Repeat this process with the remaining dates.

4. Remove the dates from the fryer and allow to cool on a wire rack for 5 minutes before serving.

NUTRITION PER SERVING

Total fat **3g**	Cholesterol **9mg**	Carbohydrates **11g**	Sugars **9g**
Saturated fat **1g**	Sodium **83mg**	Dietary fiber **1g**	Protein **3g**

129 CALORIES PER SERVING

MAKES **8**
SERVING SIZE **2**
PREP TIME **20 minutes**
COOK TIME **5 minutes**
FRYER TEMP **360°F**

Cheese lovers adore fried mozzarella. Using part-skim mozzarella cheese for these sticks cuts the fat but still makes crispy, cheesy, salty, stretchy goodness.

Mozzarella Sticks

¼ cup panko breadcrumbs

2 TB. seasoned breadcrumbs

¼ cup all-purpose flour

1 large egg, beaten

4 part-skim mozzarella cheese sticks

1 cup marinara sauce (see page 98)

1. Preheat the air fryer to 360°F.

2. In a small bowl, combine the panko and seasoned breadcrumbs, then place the flour, egg, and breadcrumb mixture into 3 separate shallow bowls.

3. Cut the cheese sticks in half, dredge in the flour, then the egg, and finally the breadcrumb mixture. Place the coated sticks on a plate, then place the plate in the freezer for 10 minutes.

4. Place a piece of parchment paper on the bottom of the fryer basket, then place the sticks on top. Cook for 5–6 minutes or until crispy and golden brown.

5. Remove the mozzarella sticks from the fryer and allow to cool on a wire rack for 5 minutes before serving with the marinara sauce on the side for dipping.

If you order this appetizer at a chain restaurant, it might have more than 700 calories!

NUTRITION PER SERVING

| Total fat **6g** | Cholesterol **34mg** | Carbohydrates **9g** | Sugars **6g** |
| Saturated fat **3g** | Sodium **337mg** | Dietary fiber **1g** | Protein **9g** |

Get any party started with a batch of this munchable snack mix. It's loaded with heart-healthy fats and has just enough heat for even the most discerning palate.

156 CALORIES PER SERVING

MAKES **4 cups**
SERVING SIZE **⅓ cup**
PREP TIME **10 minutes**
COOK TIME **5 minutes**
FRYER TEMP **360°F**

Cayenne Sesame Mix

1 TB. buttery spread, melted

2 tsp. honey

¼ tsp. cayenne pepper

2 tsp. sesame seeds

¼ tsp. kosher salt

¼ tsp. freshly ground black pepper

1 cup cashews

1 cup almonds

1 cup mini pretzels

1 cup rice squares cereal

1. Preheat the air fryer to 360°F.

2. In a large bowl, combine the buttery spread, honey, cayenne pepper, sesame seeds, kosher salt, and black pepper, then add the cashews, almonds, pretzels, and rice squares, tossing to coat.

3. Spray the air fryer baking pan with nonstick cooking spray, then pour the mixture into the pan and cook for 2 minutes.

4. Remove the sesame mix from the fryer and allow to cool in the pan on a wire rack for 5 minutes before serving. (Store in an airtight container for up to 3 days.)

NUTRITION PER SERVING

Total fat **12g**	Cholesterol **0mg**	Carbohydrates **9g**	Sugars **2g**
Saturated fat **2g**	Sodium **81mg**	Dietary fiber **2g**	Protein **5g**

Serve this delightful finger food as an appetizer or first course and your guests will swoon. Look for narrow spears of asparagus and thin slices of prosciutto.

Asparagus with Crispy Prosciutto

85 CALORIES PER SERVING

MAKES **12 bundles**
SERVING SIZE **2 bundles**
PREP TIME **15 minutes**
COOK TIME **16–24 minutes**
FRYER TEMP **360°F**

12 asparagus spears, woody ends trimmed

24 pieces thinly sliced prosciutto

1. Preheat the air fryer to 360°F.

2. Wrap each asparagus spear with 2 slices of prosciutto, then repeat this process with the remaining asparagus and prosciutto.

3. Spray the fryer basket with nonstick cooking spray, then place 2–3 bundles in the basket and cook for 4 minutes. Repeat this process with the remaining asparagus bundles.

4. Remove the bundles from the fryer and allow to cool on a wire rack for 5 minutes before serving.

NUTRITION PER SERVING

Total fat **4g**	Cholesterol **20mg**	Carbohydrates **2g**	Sugars **1g**
Saturated fat **1g**	Sodium **692mg**	Dietary fiber **1g**	Protein **11g**

109 CALORIES PER SERVING

MAKES **8**
SERVING SIZE **2**
PREP TIME **10 minutes**
COOK TIME **10 minutes**
FRYER TEMP **360°F**

This might seem like a fancy appetizer, but simple ingredients and quick prep will turn these mushrooms into one of your favorite snacking staples.

Stuffed Mushrooms

1 TB. olive oil

2 TB. grated Parmesan cheese

1 TB. fresh parsley, chopped

¼ cup panko breadcrumbs

⅛ tsp. freshly ground black pepper

8 baby portobello mushrooms, stems removed

1. Preheat the air fryer to 360°F.

2. In a large bowl, combine the olive oil, Parmesan cheese, parsley, panko breadcrumbs, and black pepper.

3. Spray the air fryer baking pan with nonstick cooking spray, then spoon the filling into each baby portobello mushroom and place the mushrooms in the pan. Cook for 10 minutes or until tender.

4. Allow the mushrooms to cool in the pan in the fryer for 10 minutes. Serve warm.

Buying this appetizer at a restaurant will cost you almost 400 calories!

NUTRITION PER SERVING

Total fat **7g**	Cholesterol **6mg**	Carbohydrates **8g**	Sugars **1g**
Saturated fat **2g**	Sodium **110mg**	Dietary fiber **1g**	Protein **5g**

Soft and herbaceous bites of this bread are simply addictive. Serve this with a salad and one of the healthy pizzas featured in this book.

157 CALORIES PER SERVING

MAKES **1 loaf**
SERVING SIZE **¼ loaf**
PREP TIME **20 minutes**
COOK TIME **10 minutes**
FRYER TEMP **360°F**

Pull-Apart Parmesan & Thyme Bread

6 oz. pizza dough
(see page 52)

1 TB. buttery spread, melted

1 tsp. dried thyme leaves

3 TB. grated Parmesan cheese

1. Preheat the air fryer to 360°F.

2. Flatten the pizza dough and cut into ¾-inch pieces.

3. In a medium bowl, combine the buttery spread, thyme, and Parmesan cheese, then roll each piece of dough in the cheese mixture.

4. Spray the air fryer baking pan with nonstick cooking spray, then place the pieces in the pan and cook for 10 minutes.

5. Remove the bread from the fryer and allow to cool in the pan on a wire rack for 10 minutes before serving.

Save about 150 calories from typical garlic bread.

NUTRITION PER SERVING

Total fat **4g**	Cholesterol **3mg**	Carbohydrates **25g**	Sugars **1g**
Saturated fat **1g**	Sodium **235mg**	Dietary fiber **1g**	Protein **5g**

(LESS) SINFUL DESSERTS

Whether you desire cake, cobbler, or even donuts (yes, donuts!), the recipes in this chapter will satisfy any sweet tooth—all made lighter and faster in the air fryer.

244 CALORIES PER SERVING

MAKES **4 pieces**
SERVING SIZE **1 piece**
PREP TIME **15 minutes**
COOK TIME **15 minutes**
FRYER TEMP **300°F**

Strawberry shortcake is one of the best desserts ever! And by using the air fryer, you can make—and enjoy— this summertime favorite quicker than baking!

Strawberry Shortcake

2 cups fresh strawberries, sliced

1 TB. granulated sugar (plus 2 tsp.)

1 cup all-purpose flour

1 tsp. baking powder

¼ tsp. baking soda

¼ tsp. kosher salt

3 TB. cold unsalted butter, diced

½ cup low-fat buttermilk

Whipped cream (for serving)

1. Preheat the air fryer to 300°F.

2. In a medium bowl, combine the strawberries and 2 teaspoons of granulated sugar. Set aside.

3. In a separate medium bowl, whisk together the 1 tablespoon of granulated sugar, all-purpose flour, baking powder, baking soda, and kosher salt. Add the butter, then use clean hands or a pastry cutter to combine the ingredients and break the butter into small pieces.

4. Slowly pour in the buttermilk, combining with your hands until the dough comes together. (It will be sticky.)

5. Spray the air fryer baking pan with nonstick cooking spray, then pour the mixture into the pan, spreading and pressing it into an even layer.

6. Cook for 15 minutes or until golden brown.

7. Remove the shortcake from the fryer and allow to cool on a wire rack for 10 minutes, then add the strawberries and 2 tablespoons of whipped cream on top before cutting and serving.

This recipe is short on calories—more than 100 fewer than traditional shortcake.

NUTRITION PER SERVING

Total fat **12g**	Cholesterol **34mg**	Carbohydrates **31g**	Sugars **7g**
Saturated fat **7g**	Sodium **371mg**	Dietary fiber **2g**	Protein **5g**

This recipe has simple but impactful ingredients that will allow you to keep enjoying a decadent dessert without sacrificing flavor—and saving calories!

Maple & Bourbon Bread Pudding

3 slices whole grain bread (preferably a day old), cubed

1 large egg

1 cup whole milk

2 TB. bourbon

½ tsp. vanilla extract

¼ cup maple syrup, divided

½ tsp. ground cinnamon

2 tsp. sparkling sugar

1. Preheat the air fryer to 270°F.

2. Spray the air fryer baking pan with nonstick cooking spray, then place the bread cubes in the pan.

3. In a medium bowl, whisk together the egg, milk, bourbon, vanilla extract, 3 tablespoons of maple syrup, and cinnamon. Pour the egg mixture over the bread and press down with a spatula to make sure to coat all the bread, then sprinkle the sparkling sugar on top and cook for 20 minutes.

4. Remove the pudding from the fryer and allow to cool in the pan on a wire rack for 10 minutes. Drizzle the remaining 1 tablespoon of maple syrup on top. Slice and serve warm.

Some versions of this classic treat have more than 500 calories per serving!

NUTRITION PER SERVING

Total fat **4g**	Cholesterol **47mg**	Carbohydrates **25g**	Sugars **16g**
Saturated fat **2g**	Sodium **154mg**	Dietary fiber **2g**	Protein **6g**

A no-fail brownie recipe for chocolate cravings is a must. This version uses applesauce to cut back on the fat and sea salt to enhance the chocolate taste.

Sea Salt Brownies

182 CALORIES PER SERVING

MAKES **8**
SERVING SIZE **1**
PREP TIME **10 minutes**
COOK TIME **15 minutes**
FRYER TEMP **300°F**

¼ cup unsweetened cocoa powder

¼ cup all-purpose flour

¼ tsp. kosher salt

½ tsp. baking powder

3 TB. unsalted butter, melted

½ cup granulated sugar

1 large egg

3 TB. unsweetened applesauce

¼ cup miniature semisweet chocolate chips

Coarse sea salt

1. Preheat the air fryer to 300°F.

2. In a large bowl, whisk together the cocoa powder, all-purpose flour, kosher salt, and baking powder.

3. In a separate large bowl, combine the butter, granulated sugar, egg, and applesauce, then use a spatula to fold in the cocoa powder mixture and the chocolate chips until well combined.

4. Spray the air fryer baking pan with nonstick cooking spray, then pour the mixture into the pan. Cook for 15 minutes or until a toothpick comes out clean when inserted in the middle.

5. Remove the brownies from the fryer, sprinkle some coarse sea salt on top, and allow to cool in the pan on a wire rack for 20 minutes before cutting and serving.

This lighter brownie can save you more than 100 calories per serving.

NUTRITION PER SERVING

Total fat **5g**	Cholesterol **35mg**	Carbohydrates **19g**	Sugars **14g**
Saturated fat **3g**	Sodium **80mg**	Dietary fiber **1g**	Protein **2g**

131 CALORIES PER SERVING

MAKES **12**
SERVING SIZE **1**
PREP TIME **90 minutes**
COOK TIME **20 minutes**
FRYER TEMP **360°F**

You don't need a drive-thru breakfast when you can make homemade donuts! Make the dough the night before and pop the donuts in the air fryer before work.

Glazed Donuts with Sprinkles

¼ cup warm water

1 tsp. dry active yeast

3 TB. granulated sugar (plus 1 tsp.)

2 cups all-purpose flour (plus extra for rolling)

½ tsp. baking powder

¼ tsp. kosher salt

1 TB. buttery spread, melted

½ cup whole milk (plus 1 TB. for the glaze)

⅔ cup confectioners' sugar

Rainbow sprinkles (for decorating)

Not cooking these donuts in a vat of hot oil will save almost 200 calories.

1. In a small bowl, combine the water, dry active yeast, and 1 teaspoon of granulated sugar. Allow the mixture to rest for 10 minutes while the yeast activates.

2. In the large bowl of a stand mixer fitted with a dough hook, combine the 3 tablespoons of granulated sugar, all-purpose flour, baking powder, and kosher salt. Pour in the yeast mixture, buttery spread, and ½ cup of milk, stirring until the dough pulls away from the sides of the bowl.

3. Cover the dough bowl with a clean dish towel and set aside for 30 minutes or until the dough doubles in size.

4. Roll out the dough on a lightly floured surface and use two 3½-inch ring molds to cut out the donuts. Set the donuts aside to rest for 20 more minutes.

5. Preheat the air fryer to 360°F.

6. Spray the fryer basket with nonstick cooking spray, then place 3 donuts in the basket and cook for 4 minutes. Repeat this process with the remaining donuts.

7. While the donuts cook, make the glaze in a small bowl by whisking together the confectioners' sugar and 1 tablespoon of milk until smooth.

8. Remove the donuts from the fryer and place on a wire rack to cool for 5 minutes, then dip in the glaze and top with the sprinkles. Set aside for 20 minutes before serving.

NUTRITION PER SERVING

Total fat **2g**	Cholesterol **1mg**	Carbohydrates **27g**	Sugars **11g**
Saturated fat **1g**	Sodium **60mg**	Dietary fiber **0g**	Protein **3g**

115 CALORIES
PER SERVING

MAKES **30**
SERVING SIZE **3**
PREP TIME **60 minutes**
COOK TIME **13–21 minutes**
FRYER TEMP **360°F**

This gluten-free treat will please any sweet tooth.
Even if you're not on a gluten-free diet, you won't
be able to resist these delicious treats!

Gluten-Free Donut Holes

¼ cup warm water

1 tsp. dry active yeast

4 tsp. granulated sugar, divided

2 cups gluten-free baking mix

½ tsp. baking powder

¼ tsp. kosher salt

1 TB. buttery spread, melted

½ cup whole milk

¼ cup semisweet chocolate chips

1. In a medium bowl, combine the warm water, dry active yeast, and 1 teaspoon of granulated sugar and allow to rest for 10 minutes for the yeast to activate.

2. In the large bowl of a stand mixer fitted with a dough hook, combine 3 teaspoons of granulated sugar, gluten-free baking mix, baking powder, and kosher salt.

3. Pour the yeast mixture, buttery spread, and milk into the dough mixture and stir until the dough pulls away from the bowl. Set aside to rest for 30 minutes.

4. Preheat the air fryer to 360°F.

5. Roll out the dough between 2 pieces of parchment paper until it's ¾-inch thick, then use a small ring mold to cut out 30 small circles.

6. Spray the fryer basket with nonstick cooking spray, then place 8–10 pieces in the basket and cook for 4 minutes or until puffed and golden brown. Repeat this process with the remaining dough pieces.

7. Remove the donut holes from the fryer and allow to cool on a wire rack for 10 minutes.

8. While the holes cool, place the semisweet chocolate chips in a medium microwave-safe bowl and cook in the microwave for 1 minute or until melted. Dip each hole in the chocolate, return to the wire rack, and allow to cool for 5 minutes before serving.

Eliminate more than 100 calories compared with fast-food donut holes.

NUTRITION PER SERVING

Total fat **1g**	Cholesterol **1mg**	Carbohydrates **5g**	Sugars **5g**
Saturated fat **0g**	Sodium **65mg**	Dietary fiber **0g**	Protein **2g**

Fried dough and cannolis are famous belly-busting fare—but they don't have to be. Air-fried dough and a lightened-up dip make this a healthier choice.

99 CALORIES PER SERVING

MAKES **16**
SERVING SIZE **2**
PREP TIME **10 minutes**
COOK TIME **10 minutes**
FRYER TEMP **390°F**

Zeppole with Cannoli Dip

½ cup all-purpose flour

1¼ tsp. baking powder

2 TB. granulated sugar

Pinch of kosher salt

½ cup whole milk ricotta cheese

1 large egg, beaten

¼ tsp. vanilla extract

1 tsp. confectioners' sugar

For the dip:

¼ cup whole milk ricotta cheese

¼ tsp. vanilla extract

2 TB. nonfat vanilla Greek yogurt

1 TB. miniature semisweet chocolate chips

1. Preheat the air fryer to 390°F.

2. In a medium bowl, whisk together the all-purpose flour, baking powder, granulated sugar, and kosher salt, then add the ricotta cheese, egg, and vanilla extract, stirring until a thick batter forms.

3. Spray the air fryer basket with nonstick cooking spray, then place 8 individual tablespoons of batter into the basket and cook for 5 minutes or until puffed and golden brown. Repeat this process with the remaining batter.

4. While the zeppole cook, make the dip in a small bowl by combining the ricotta cheese, vanilla extract, vanilla Greek yogurt, and miniature semisweet chocolate chips. Set aside.

5. Remove the zeppole from the fryer and allow to cool on a wire rack for 10 minutes, then dust with the confectioners' sugar and serve with the dip.

NUTRITION PER SERVING

Total fat **2g**	Cholesterol **35mg**	Carbohydrates **11g**	Sugars **5g**
Saturated fat **2g**	Sodium **107mg**	Dietary fiber **0g**	Protein **5g**

Lighten up a plain apple turnover by using airy phyllo dough—and then amp up the flavor with a pop of pumpkin pie spice.

Apple Turnovers

119 CALORIES PER SERVING

MAKES **4**
SERVING SIZE **1**
PREP TIME **30 minutes**
COOK TIME **10 minutes**
FRYER TEMP **330°F**

1 Granny Smith apple, peeled, quartered, and thinly sliced

½ tsp. pumpkin pie spice

Juice of ½ lemon

1 TB. granulated sugar

Pinch of kosher salt

6 sheets phyllo dough

1. Preheat the air fryer to 330°F.

2. In a medium bowl, combine the apple, pumpkin pie spice, lemon juice, granulated sugar, and kosher salt.

3. Cut the phyllo dough sheets into 4 equal pieces and place individual tablespoons of apple filling in the center of each piece, then fold in both sides and roll from front to back.

4. Spray the fryer basket with nonstick cooking spray, then place the turnovers in the basket and cook for 10 minutes or until golden brown.

5. Remove the turnovers from the fryer and allow to cool on a wire rack for 10 minutes before serving.

Classic deep-fried apple turnovers usually have 250–300 calories.

NUTRITION PER SERVING

Total fat **2g**	Cholesterol **0mg**	Carbohydrates **24g**	Sugars **7g**
Saturated fat **0g**	Sodium **173mg**	Dietary fiber **1g**	Protein **2g**

MAKES **8**
SERVING SIZE **1**
PREP TIME **90 minutes**
COOK TIME **28–40 minutes**
FRYER TEMP **360°F**

These miniature desserts are worth the effort. Lightly sweetened fruit wrapped in a flaky (but not greasy) pastry makes these pies a perfectly portioned treat.

Miniature Frosted Pies

For the crust:

1 cup all-purpose flour (plus extra for kneading)

½ tsp. kosher salt

1 tsp. granulated sugar

6 TB. cold unsalted butter, diced

1–2 TB. ice water

For the filling:

½ cup frozen wild blueberries

1 TB. granulated sugar

2 TB. water mixed with ¾ tsp. cornstarch

For the frosting:

¼ cup confectioners' sugar

2 TB. low-fat milk

1. Make the crust in a food processor by pulsing the all-purpose flour, kosher salt, and granulated sugar. Add the butter and pulse it into small pieces, then add the ice water 1 teaspoon at a time until the dough forms a ball.

2. Place the dough on a lightly floured surface and gently form into a disc. Wrap in plastic wrap and refrigerate for 1 hour.

3. Preheat the air fryer to 360°F.

4. While the dough chills, make the filling in a medium microwave-safe bowl by combining the blueberries, granulated sugar, and cornstarch mixture. Cook in the microwave for 2 minutes, stir, and cook for 2 more minutes.

5. Place the dough between 2 pieces of parchment paper and roll into a rectangle. Use a knife to divide the dough into 8 smaller rectangles, then place individual tablespoons of filling on each piece and fold in half over the filling. Use a fork to press and seal the edges and to poke a few holes in the top.

6. Spray the fryer basket with nonstick cooking spray, then place 3–4 pies in the basket and cook for 12 minutes or until golden brown. Repeat this process with the remaining pies.

7. While the pies cook, make the frosting in a small bowl by combining the confectioners' sugar and milk.

8. Remove the pies from the fryer, place on a wire rack, spoon the frosting on top, and allow to cool for 10–15 minutes before serving.

NUTRITION PER SERVING

Total fat **8g**	Cholesterol **23mg**	Carbohydrates **18g**	Sugars **6g**
Saturated fat **5g**	Sodium **72mg**	Dietary fiber **1g**	Protein **2g**

These handheld fruit fritters are simply irresistible. Make a large batch and store them in the freezer to enjoy autumn flavors all winter—or all year—long.

Apple Cider Fritters

112 CALORIES PER SERVING

MAKES **24**
SERVING SIZE **2**
PREP TIME **20 minutes**
COOK TIME **48 minutes**
FRYER TEMP **360°F**

½ cup apple cider

½ cup granulated sugar

2 TB. coconut oil, melted

1 large egg, beaten

¼ cup buttermilk

1 cup all-purpose flour

¾ cup whole wheat pastry flour

1 tsp. baking powder

¾ tsp. ground cinnamon

⅛ tsp. ground nutmeg

¼ tsp. kosher salt

1 small Gala apple, peeled and finely chopped

1 TB. confectioners' sugar

1. Pour the apple cider into a small saucepan and bring to a boil, then reduce to a simmer and cook until reduced by half. Set aside to cool.

2. In a large bowl, whisk together the cider, granulated sugar, coconut oil, egg, and buttermilk. Stir in the all-purpose flour, whole wheat pastry flour, baking powder, ground cinnamon, ground nutmeg, and kosher salt, then fold in the chopped apple. Cover the bowl and refrigerate for 20 minutes.

3. Preheat the air fryer to 360°F.

4. Spray the air fryer baking pan with nonstick cooking spray, then place 4 individual tablespoons of dough in the pan and cook for 8 minutes or until puffy and golden brown. Repeat this process with the remaining dough.

5. Remove the fritters from the fryer and allow to cool on a wire rack for 10 minutes, then dust with the confectioners' sugar before serving.

A fritter from a bakery will often have 400 calories and 20 grams of fat!

NUTRITION PER SERVING

Total fat **3g**	Cholesterol **16mg**	Carbohydrates **20g**	Sugars **10g**
Saturated fat **2g**	Sodium **79mg**	Dietary fiber **1g**	Protein **2g**

These muffins certainly taste decadent, but natural sweetness from applesauce and banana mean less sugar in this recipe, but you won't miss it.

Banana Muffins with Semisweet Chocolate Chips

½ cup all-purpose flour

½ cup whole wheat pastry flour

¾ tsp. baking powder

¼ tsp. baking soda

¼ tsp. ground cinnamon

½ tsp. kosher salt

½ cup granulated sugar

1 large egg, beaten

¼ cup canola oil

1 large banana, mashed

¼ cup unsweetened applesauce

1 tsp. vanilla extract

⅓ cup semisweet chocolate chips

1. Preheat the air fryer to 330°F.

2. In a large bowl, combine the all-purpose flour, whole wheat pastry flour, baking powder, baking soda, ground cinnamon, and kosher salt. Set aside.

3. In a separate large bowl, combine the granulated sugar, egg, canola oil, banana, unsweetened applesauce, and vanilla extract.

4. Add the banana mixture to the flour mixture, stirring gently until combined, then fold in the chocolate chips.

5. Spray eight 3-inch ramekins with nonstick cooking spray, then pour equal amounts of the banana mixture into the ramekins.

6. Place 2–3 ramekins in the fryer basket and cook for 20 minutes or until a toothpick comes out clean when inserted in the middle. Repeat this process with the remaining ramekins.

7. Remove the ramekins from the fryer and allow to cool on a wire rack for 20 minutes before serving.

NUTRITION PER SERVING

Total fat **10g**	Cholesterol **23mg**	Carbohydrates **34g**	Sugars **21g**
Saturated fat **2g**	Sodium **106mg**	Dietary fiber **2g**	Protein **3g**

164 CALORIES
PER SERVING

MAKES **4 pieces**
SERVING SIZE **1 piece**
PREP TIME **10 minutes**
COOK TIME **15 minutes**
FRYER TEMP **360°F**

This rustic dessert only looks difficult to make. You can create this summertime classic with almost nothing more than frozen peaches and pantry staples.

Classic Peach Cobbler

2 cups frozen peaches

2 TB. granulated sugar, divided

Juice of ½ lemon

½ tsp. cornstarch

½ cup all-purpose flour

½ tsp. baking powder

¼ tsp. baking soda

¼ tsp. kosher salt

2 TB. unsalted butter, diced

¼ cup low-fat buttermilk

1. Preheat the air fryer to 360°F.

2. Spray the air fryer baking pan with nonstick cooking spray, then place the peaches, 1 tablespoon of granulated sugar, lemon juice, and cornstarch in the pan, tossing to combine. Set aside.

3. In a large bowl, combine 1 tablespoon of granulated sugar, all-purpose flour, baking powder, baking soda, and kosher salt. Add the unsalted butter, then use a fork or a pastry cutter to cut it into the flour mixture.

4. Pour in the buttermilk and stir until a soft dough forms.

5. Place large pieces of dough evenly over the peaches and cook for 15 minutes.

6. Allow to cool in the pan in the fryer for 10 minutes. Serve warm.

Peach cobbler at your favorite restaurant will tip the scales at 500 calories!

NUTRITION PER SERVING

Total fat **6g**	Cholesterol **16mg**	Carbohydrates **26g**	Sugars **14g**
Saturated fat **4g**	Sodium **130mg**	Dietary fiber **1g**	Protein **3g**

This decadent chocolate cake is rich but still lighter than most similar variations. Made with six simple ingredients, this will beat anything from a box!

Chocolate Lava Cakes

290 CALORIES PER SERVING

MAKES **4**
SERVING SIZE **1**
PREP TIME **10 minutes**
COOK TIME **21 minutes**
FRYER TEMP **360°F**

4 TB. unsalted butter

2 oz. semisweet chocolate chips

2 large eggs

⅓ cup granulated sugar

¼ cup all-purpose flour

⅛ tsp. kosher salt

1. Preheat the air fryer to 360°F.

2. Place the butter and chocolate chips in a medium microwave-safe bowl and cook in the microwave for 1 minute. Set aside to cool slightly.

3. In a medium bowl, whisk together the eggs and granulated sugar, then stir in the chocolate mixture.

4. Gently fold in the all-purpose flour and kosher salt, stirring again until just combined.

5. Spray four 3-inch ramekins with nonstick cooking spray, then pour the mixture into the ramekins. Place 2 ramekins in the fryer basket and cook for 10 minutes. Repeat this process with the remaining ramekins.

6. Remove the ramekins from the fryer and allow to cool on a wire rack for 10 minutes. Serve warm.

Everyone loves chocolate cake, but now you can avoid the 400-calorie versions.

NUTRITION PER SERVING

Total fat **18g**	Cholesterol **124mg**	Carbohydrates **31g**	Sugars **24g**
Saturated fat **11g**	Sodium **74mg**	Dietary fiber **1g**	Protein **5g**

A crisp is one of the easiest and most spectacular desserts you can make. Juicy fruit, warm spices, and a bit of crunch will please any sweet tooth.

Pear Crisp with Pistachios

160 CALORIES PER SERVING

MAKES **4 ramekins**
SERVING SIZE **1 ramekin**
PREP TIME **15 minutes**
COOK TIME **40 minutes**
FRYER TEMP **330°F**

2 medium pears, peeled and chopped

Juice of ½ lemon

1 tsp. cornstarch

3 TB. granulated sugar, divided

½ tsp. ground cinnamon, divided

¼ cup rolled oats

1 TB. all-purpose flour

1 TB. coconut oil

3 TB. pistachios, chopped

1. Preheat the air fryer to 330°F.

2. In a medium bowl, combine the pears, lemon juice, cornstarch, 1 tablespoon of granulated sugar, and 1 tablespoon of ground cinnamon. Set aside.

3. Make the topping in a separate medium bowl by using a fork to mash together the 2 tablespoons of granulated sugar, ¼ teaspoon of ground cinnamon, rolled oats, all-purpose flour, coconut oil, ground cinnamon, granulated sugar, and pistachios.

4. Spray four 3-inch ramekins with nonstick cooking spray, then transfer the pear mixture to the ramekins and sprinkle the topping on top. Place 2 ramekins in the fryer basket and cook for 20 minutes or until the topping is golden brown and the fruit bubbles. Repeat this process with the remaining ramekins.

5. Remove the ramekins from the fryer and allow to cool on a wire rack for 10 minutes before serving.

NUTRITION PER SERVING

Total fat **6g**	Cholesterol **0mg**	Carbohydrates **26g**	Sugars **16g**
Saturated fat **3g**	Sodium **18mg**	Dietary fiber **4g**	Protein **2g**

260 CALORIES
PER SERVING

MAKES **8**
SERVING SIZE **1**
PREP TIME **30 minutes**
COOK TIME **15 minutes**
FRYER TEMP **360°F**

Cookies meet oat bars in this dessert combination.
These delectable treats are loaded with whole grain
goodness but still taste sweet and delicious.

Oatmeal Raisin Cookie Bars

⅓ cup all-purpose flour

¼ tsp. kosher salt

¼ tsp. baking powder

¼ tsp. ground cinnamon

¼ cup light brown sugar, lightly packed

¼ cup granulated sugar

½ cup canola oil

1 large egg

1 tsp. vanilla extract

1⅓ cups quick-cook oats

⅓ cup raisins

1. Preheat the air fryer to 360°F.

2. In a large bowl, combine the all-purpose flour, kosher salt, baking powder, ground cinnamon, light brown sugar, granulated sugar, canola oil, egg, vanilla extract, quick-cook oats, and raisins.

3. Spray the air fryer baking pan with nonstick cooking spray, then pour the oat mixture into the pan and press down to evenly distribute. Cook for 15 minutes or until golden brown.

4. Remove from the fryer and allow to cool in the pan on a wire rack for 20 minutes before slicing and serving.

NUTRITION PER SERVING

Total fat **15g**	Cholesterol **23mg**	Carbohydrates **30g**	Sugars **16g**
Saturated fat **1g**	Sodium **60mg**	Dietary fiber **2g**	Protein **3g**

Plain bananas can make a wildly decadent dessert you can feel good about eating. Serve them with a side of frozen Greek yogurt or with fresh strawberries.

Roasted Bananas

MAKES **4 pieces**
SERVING SIZE **2 pieces**
PREP TIME **10 minutes**
COOK TIME **10 minutes**
FRYER TEMP **300°F**

3 TB. water

1 TB. light brown sugar

1 banana

1. Preheat the air fryer to 300°F.

2. Spray the air fryer baking pan with nonstick cooking spray, then combine the water and light brown sugar in the pan.

3. Cut the banana in half and split each piece lengthwise, then place the banana pieces cut side down in the pan and cook for 10 minutes.

4. Remove the bananas from the fryer and allow to cool in the pan on a wire rack for 10 minutes before serving.

NUTRITION PER SERVING

Total fat **0g**	Cholesterol **0mg**	Carbohydrates **19g**	Sugars **13g**
Saturated fat **0g**	Sodium **1mg**	Dietary fiber **2g**	Protein **1g**

99 CALORIES
PER SERVING

MAKES **18**
SERVING SIZE **2**
PREP TIME **10 minutes**
COOK TIME **9–20 minutes**
FRYER TEMP **330°F**

These delicate twists have a touch of sweetness
and are just as airy and delicious as their deep-fried
counterparts, but they lack extra oil and saturated fat.

Cinnamon Sugar Twists

1 sheet puff pastry

¼ cup granulated sugar

1 tsp. ground cinnamon

1. Preheat the air fryer to 330°F.

2. Cut the puff pastry sheet into 18 small strips and gently twist each piece to create a spiral shape.

3. Spray the fryer basket with nonstick cooking spray, then place 5–6 twists in the basket and cook for 3–5 minutes or until golden brown. Repeat this process with the remaining twists.

4. While the twists cook, combine the granulated sugar and ground cinnamon in a shallow dish.

5. Remove the twists from the fryer, tossing in the cinnamon sugar mixture, and allow to cool on a wire rack for 5 minutes before serving.

Fried dough with cinnamon sugar will cost you more than 300 calories and 20 grams of fat.

NUTRITION PER SERVING

| Total fat **5g** | Cholesterol **0mg** | Carbohydrates **12g** | Sugars **6g** |
| Saturated fat **1g** | Sodium **35mg** | Dietary fiber **0g** | Protein **1g** |

Index

Publisher Mike Sanders
Associate Publisher Billy Fields
Senior Editor Brook Farling
Editor Christopher Stolle
Design and Art Direction William Thomas
Photographer Kelley Jordan Schuyler
Food Stylist Savannah Norris
Prepress Technician Brian Massey
Proofreader Monica Stone
Indexer Celia McCoy

First American Edition, 2017
Published in the United States by DK Publishing
6081 E. 82nd Street, Indianapolis, Indiana 46250

Copyright © 2017 Dorling Kindersley Limited

A Penguin Random House Company

17 18 19 20   10 9 8 7 6 5 4 3 2 1

001–306714–September/2017

Published in the United States
by Dorling Kindersley Limited

ISBN: 9781465464873
Library of Congress Catalog Card Number: 2017933256

Printed and bound in China

All images © Dorling Kindersley Limited
For further information see: www.dkimages.com

A WORLD OF IDEAS:
SEE ALL THERE IS TO KNOW
www.dk.com